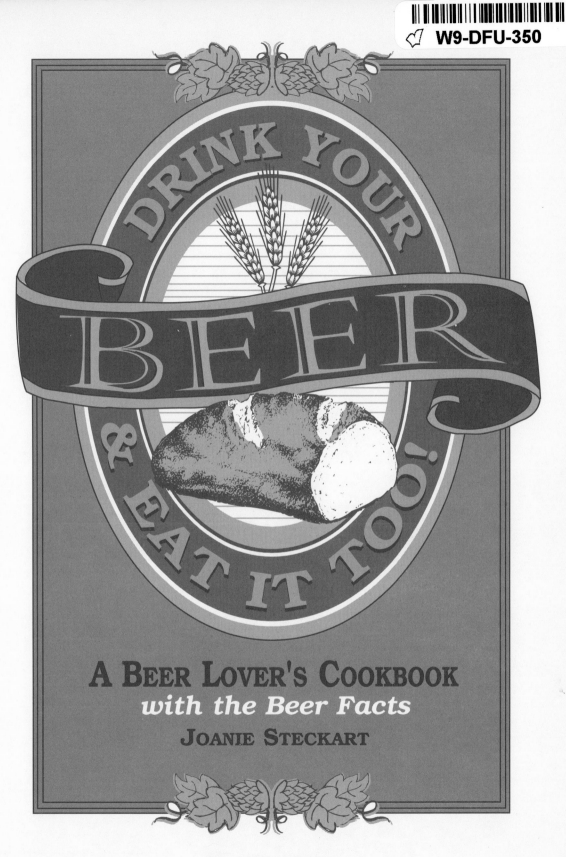

DRINK YOUR

BEER

& EAT IT TOO!

A BEER LOVER'S COOKBOOK
with the Beer Facts
JOANIE STECKART

NOB HILL PRESS
DePere, Wisconsin

First edition

Library of Congress Catalog Number: 95-67564

ISBN: 0-9645006-0-4

Published by
Nob Hill Press
2998 Heritage Road
DePere, Wisconsin 54115

Printed by
Palmer Publications, Inc.
P.O. Box 296
Amherst, Wisconsin 54406

DEDICATION

I dedicate this book to my parents, my husband John, children Jolie, John, Jr. and Jillisa and to all those who supported me in getting it together. Some gave me recipes, others gave me moral support and especially those who tasted and tested.

A special thank you to the one who made it reality —

Book from
Karin
a Xmas gift —

TABLE OF CONTENTS

You say,

"Why do you write a cookbook using beer as an ingredient in each recipe?"

I answer,

"It's my parents' fault. I'm a victim of my early environment."

You say,

"Come now, in this day and age, you have to take responsibility for your own actions."

I repeat,

"It's my parents' fault. My mom liked to cook and my dad liked a beer. I'm a combination of my mom and dad."

My dad liked to relax with a beer after work, and my mom liked to try new and innovative recipes. When she found a recipe for beer bread and another for chocolate cake using beer, she was intrigued. Mom didn't go into the liquor store for her beer, but going to the supermarket and checking out a six-pack with her baking supplies was very acceptable.

As new recipes using beer were found, my dad began hanging around the kitchen because he believed in the old adage, "Waste not, want not"; he especially liked the recipes that used only partial cans or bottles of beer.

So you see, it is my parents' fault, and I am a victim of my early environment. I like to cook and I like a beer.

The Story of Beer

The origin of beer is lost somewhere in the stone age, long before history was recorded. Anthropologists can only guess how it happened, and their guesswork goes something like this: once, in a camp of some nomadic hunter-gatherers, there was a supply of wild grain, painstakingly collected for food. Somehow, possibly in a sudden summer rainstorm, a pool of warm water formed where the grain was stored. In a short time, the grain fermented, turning the water into a thick, dark liquid. Some adventurous soul among these primitive people sampled the liquid and found that it tasted good.

Man had discovered beer.

From that time to the present, beer has been an important part of life in virtually every society on earth.

According to one prominent anthropologist, what lured our ancient ancestors out of their caves may not have been a thirst for knowledge but a thirst for beer.

There is a theory that when man learned to ferment grain into beer it became one of his most important sources of nutrition. Beer has more protein than unfermented grain, and it also tasted better than unfermented grain.

In order to have a steady supply of beer, it was necessary to have a steady supply of beer's ingredients. Man had to give up his nomadic ways, settle down, and begin farming. Once he did, civilization was just a stone's throw away.

After civilization got rolling, beer was always an important part of it. Noah carried beer on the ark; Sumerian laborers received rations of it. Egyptians made it from barley, Babylonians made it from wheat, and Incas made it from corn.

And, so it went, through the centuries. From ancient times to the present day, beer has been and is a part of celebration and good fellowship.

We hope that the recipes in *Drink Your Beer & Eat It Too* increase and promote your future celebrations and good fellowship.

APPETIZERS

1-16

CHEESE & RYE BREAD

1   round loaf rye bread
1   pound cheese spread
     (2 8-ounce jars, any flavor)
1   10³/₄-ounce can cheddar
     cheese soup
²/₃ cup beer

Cut off top of bread and hollow out, leaving about ³/₄-inch sides and bottom to loaf. Reserve bread chunks for dipping. Combine cheese spread, soup, and beer and mix well. Put into bread shell and bake at 350 degrees for about 30 minutes, or until cheese mixture is melted and bubbly; stir after first 15 minutes. Serve with chunks of bread for dipping. Bread tastes good when cheese is gone!! Serves 8-10.

If you hear that someone is in charge of "polishing" in a brewery, he is not polishing glass bottles—rather, he is filtering the beer to remove all sediment to assure its clarity and brilliance.

CHEDDAR CHEESE FONDUE

¹/₄ cup butter or margarine
¹/₄ cup flour
¹/₂ teaspoon salt
¹/₂ teaspoon dry mustard
1 12-ounce can beer
1¹/₂ teaspoons Worcestershire sauce
2 cups sharp cheddar cheese, grated
Bite-size pieces of pumpernickel bread

Melt butter or margarine in saucepan and blend in flour; add salt and dry mustard. Slowly add beer and Worcestershire sauce; continue stirring until mixture thickens and bubbles. Add cheese, stirring constantly until melted. Keep warm in fondue dish and serve with chunks of bread speared on forks. Makes approximately 2 cups.

The first breweries in America were private breweries owned by individuals; the first public brewery was started by Peter Minuit around 1632.

BEER-CHEESE DIP

2/3 cup beer
   Tabasco sauce, to taste
1 cup cubed Velveeta
   cheese spread
1 tablespoon flour
1/2 teaspoon dry mustard

In 1-quart, microwave-safe dish, combine beer and Tabasco sauce to taste. Cook, uncovered, full power 1 to 2 minutes. Meanwhile, toss together cheese cubes, flour, and mustard. Stir into beer mixture. Cook, uncovered, on high an additional 2-4 minutes until cheese is melted and mixture is heated through; stir often. Stir in enough additional beer to make a dipping consistency. Serve with crackers, chips, or vegetable dippers. Makes 1 cup.

The captain and crew of the historic Mayflower depended on beer to prevent scurvy when citrus fruits were not available. It is said the passengers landed short of their original destination because the supply of beer was running low.

MEXICAN CHEESE DIP

8 ounces cream cheese
6 ounces cheddar cheese, grated
1/2 cup beer
1 1/2 tablespoons finely chopped jalapeno pepper

In microwave-safe bowl, combine cream cheese and grated cheddar; cook at 50% power for 4-5 minutes. Stir to make sure cheese is melted. Stir in beer and peppers and cook with cover on at 50% power for an additional 6 minutes, until bubbly. Stir after the first 2 minutes and again at 4 minutes. Serve hot with crackers, chips, or vegetables. Makes 2 cups.

In 1985, breweries in the United States produced 64 billion 12-ounce servings of beer. Drink up!

5

ONION BEER DIP

8 ounces cream cheese, softened

1/3 cup beer

1 cup sour cream

1 1-ounce package onion soup mix

Whip cheese until fluffy. Add beer and beat until smooth. Stir in sour cream and soup mix. Place in refrigerator for 1 hour before serving. Mix well just before serving. Makes approximately 2 cups.

From early times to the present, beer has been an important part of life in virtually every society on earth. It was brewed by the ancient Babylonians, Egyptians, and Chinese. It has been used in religious rituals, depicted on coins, and honored in epic sagas. Through all the centuries, in moments of triumph, celebration, and fellowship, no drink has contributed more to man's enjoyment than beer.

TOMATO-BEER DIP

2 tablespoons butter
1 pound Velveeta cheese
1 egg, beaten
2/3 cup beer
1/2 10 3/4-ounce can tomato
   soup
1/2 teaspoon dry mustard
   Dash cayenne pepper
1 tablespoon Worcestershire
   sauce

Melt butter in heavy skillet over low heat; add cheese and melt slowly. In small bowl beat together egg, beer, tomato soup, dry mustard, pepper, and Worcestershire sauce. Add egg mixture to cheese mixture. Serve with chunks of French bread. Makes 3 cups.

The early Pilgrims brought beer to America because its "shelf life" was longer than that of water on the long trips across the ocean.

ROQUEFORT & BEER SPREAD

1 12-ounce can beer
1½ pounds sharp cheddar cheese, grated
2 ounces Roquefort cheese
3 tablespoons butter, melted
1 medium onion, minced
1½ teaspoons garlic powder
2 teaspoons Worcestershire sauce

Heat beer in saucepan to boiling and set aside to cool. Blend cheddar cheese, Roquefort, and butter until smooth. Add onions, garlic powder, and Worcestershire sauce, stirring well. Add beer until spreading consistency is reached. Serve with crackers and toast points. Makes 4 cups.

Fluoride's ability to help prevent tooth decay is commonly used to advertise toothpaste. Do you think we will ever hear that beer helps to prevent cavities? At a hospital in London, teeth were soaked in fourteen different liquids for a period of time; those in beer came out perfect and those in fruit juices developed cavities.

TWO-CHEESE BEER SPREAD

1 pound sharp cheddar cheese, grated
1 pound Swiss cheese, grated
3 cloves garlic, crushed
1 tablespoon Worcestershire sauce
1 teaspoon Tabasco sauce
1 12-ounce can beer (if you don't use it all—drink it!!)
1 5¾-ounce jar stuffed olives, chopped

Mix cheeses, garlic, Worcestershire sauce, and Tabasco sauce, adding beer last to moisten mixture to a spreadable consistency. If mixture becomes dry, add more beer. Add chopped olives. Serve with assorted crackers. Makes 2 cups.

Most of us associate the name of Louis Pasteur with the pasteurization of milk, but Pasteur's primary experiments were done to find a way to preserve beer and wine. He is known as "the Father of Modern Brewing."

BEER-CHEESE SPREAD

8 ounces sharp cheddar
   cheese, shredded
8 ounces processed
   American cheese,
   shredded
3 ounces cream cheese,
   softened
4 ounces blue cheese,
   crumbled
3/4 cup flat beer,
   room temperature
2 teaspoons onion juice
   (or minced onion)
1 garlic clove, crushed
1 teaspoon Tabasco sauce

Combine all ingredients; mix well. Cover and refrigerate. Serve with crackers. Makes 4 cups.

Present day food inspectors use much more sophisticated methods in checking beer than the beer testers in early Europe. Inspectors, called beer conners, entered a tavern unannounced, drew a portion of beer which they proceeded to pour on a bench. After sitting on the beer for a half hour, the beer conner stood up and the verdict was in: if his trousers stuck to the bench, the beer contained too much sugar which effects fermentation.

10

CHEESE BALL

1 pound cheddar cheese, grated

1 pound Swiss cheese, grated

1½ ounces Roquefort cheese, crumbled

2 teaspoons horseradish sauce

1 teaspoon Worcestershire sauce

1 large onion, minced

1 12-ounce can beer

½ cup chopped nuts
Minced parsley leaves

With electric mixer at low speed, blend cheeses, horseradish sauce, Worcestershire sauce, and onion together, gradually adding beer. Remove portions of cheese mixture from bowl to make size of ball desired. Form mixture into ball. (If mixture becomes difficult to handle, wrap cheese mixture in plastic wrap and refrigerate before forming ball.) Combine nuts and parsley; roll ball in mixture and refrigerate. Serve with crackers. Makes 3 5-inch balls.

At the Green Dragon Inn, a favorite tavern during the era of the American Revolution, you could order a "marrathan," which was a measure of beer with sugar added, or a more complicated combination of beer, wine, gin, egg yolks, orange peel, spices, and sugar which was called a "Rumfustian."

BEEF BEER BALLS

3　cups dry bread cubes
2¼　cups warm beer, divided
2　pounds ground beef
1　egg
2　teaspoons minced garlic
1　cup diced onion
2　tablespoons Worcestershire sauce
¼　teaspoon pepper
4　tablespoons butter or oil
1　1-ounce package onion soup mix
1　cup sour half-and-half or sour cream

Soak bread in ¾ cup warm beer. Squeeze some moisture from bread and combine with meat, egg, garlic, onion, Worcestershire sauce, and pepper. Blend well and form into bite-size balls. Melt butter in large baking dish. Place meatballs in dish and brown in 350-degree oven, about 20 minutes. Place browned meatballs into large saucepan, sprinkle with onion soup mix and remaining beer; cover and simmer approximately 10 minutes. Add sour half-and-half or sour cream and heat at low temperature until well blended. Makes 50-60 meatballs.

Christmas trees are to Christmas and chocolate rabbits are to Easter as beer is to Oktoberfest, an autumn festival much enjoyed by beer drinkers.

12

TIPSY TURKEY BALLS

2 pounds ground, skinless
    turkey
1 large onion, minced
    Salt, pepper, and garlic
    powder to taste
¼ cup water
2 cups ketchup
1 12-ounce can beer

Mix turkey, onion, and spices together and form into bite-size meatballs. In saucepan, combine water, ketchup, and beer. Bring to a boil; reduce heat and gently drop meatballs into liquid. Simmer over medium to low heat for 1 hour. Serve meatballs in chafing dish with ketchup mixture. Makes 50-60 meatballs.

In the 18th century the quality of beer was determined by its alcohol content. "X" was for weak beer, "XX" for the more commonly consumed beer, and "XXX" for the strongest beer. Today we have "light" beer and also non-alcoholic beer.

COCKTAIL DOGS

1 cup brown sugar
1 cup ketchup
1 cup beer
60 small hot dogs or
   cut pieces

Mix sugar, ketchup, and beer in medium saucepan and heat. Stir in hot dogs. Simmer until flavored. Serve in chafing dish with toothpicks. Makes 60 individual pieces.

If someone says he will "take you down a peg," it would probably be safe to say he didn't realize what he was saying. The origin of "take you down a peg" comes from beer drinkers who used notches on their drinking horns to measure who could drink the amount between notches the quickest.

BATTER FRIED CHEESE CURDS

1	cup flour
½	teaspoon baking powder
2	teaspoons peanut oil
½	cup beer
2	eggs, well beaten
40-50	cheese curds
	Cooking oil to deep fry

Combine flour, baking powder, peanut oil, beer, and eggs; blend well. Dip cheese curds in batter and drop into deep-fryer filled with about 3 inches of hot oil. Brown one side; turn and brown other side. Cook a total of 3-4 minutes. Remove with slotted spoon and drain on paper towel. May be salted lightly, if desired. Makes 40-50 appetizers.

American beers are often requested in foreign countries; yet approximately 95 percent of all beer consumed in this country is produced in the United States. "Made in America and enjoyed in America."

BATTER FRIED ONION RINGS

4	large Bermuda onions
1½	cups flour
1½	teaspoons baking powder
½	teaspoon baking soda
¼	teaspoon salt
	Pinch of sugar
1	12-ounce can beer
	Oil for deep-frying
	Salt to taste

Cut onions into ¼-inch slices. Separate into rings. Mix flour, baking powder, soda, salt, and sugar in large bowl. Stir in beer until smooth. Don't overmix!

Pour oil into deep-fryer, wok, or deep saucepan to depth of about 3 inches and heat to 375 degrees. Test oil for proper heat by putting a bread cube into the hot oil; it should become crisp and brown quickly. Remove bread cube.

Drop a few onion rings at a time into batter. Let excess batter drain off. Deep-fry until golden on all sides, about 2-3 minutes. Remove with a slotted spoon to a baking sheet lined with paper towel. Sprinkle with salt, if desired. Serve hot. Makes 50-70 individual rings.

Barley was first used to make beer because it was the least suitable grain for making bread; fortunately for beer drinkers, it makes the best beer.

BEVERAGES

17-22

BEER—
SOUTH OF THE BORDER

1 **12-ounce can cold beer**
Pinch of coarse salt
Wedge of lemon or lime

Pour beer into glass and add pinch of salt. Squeeze lemon or lime over top (add only the juice, not the rind). Drink without stirring. You can also drop the salt and juice directly into the can or bottle and drink. Serves 1.

Charlemagne, as Holy Roman Emperor in the early part of the 9th century, required monasteries to provide hospitality to travelers; the three "B's" of hospitality at that time were bed, bread, and beer.

DRINK AND TELL

1 12-ounce can frozen
    lemonade concentrate
12 ounces vodka
1 12-ounce can beer
    Ice

Use lemonade can for measuring vodka. Put lemonade, vodka, and beer in electric blender; fill with ice. Blend and serve. Serves 4.

From the eastern seaboard to the Pacific coast, beer is a traditional part of a family reunion, a day at the beach, or an afternoon at the ballpark, as well as the traditional reward for mowing the lawn, clipping the hedge, or cleaning the garage.

19

BREW-ADE PUNCH

16-20 ice cubes for pitcher
 1 12-ounce can chilled
    beer
 1 .5-ounce packet
    lemonade powder
 2 tablespoons lime juice
 2 tablespoons blue
    curacao (optional)
 4 teaspoons super fine
    sugar
 12 ounces ginger ale

Put ice cubes in 2 quart pitcher and combine all ingredients. Stir well. Pour over ice cubes in glasses. Serves 4.

Beer is a delicate product. Beer should be stored in a dark, cold place as it is sensitive to light and heat.

20

PARTY PUNCH

1 6-ounce can frozen
   lemonade concentrate
6 ounces brandy
1 12-ounce can beer
   Ice cubes

Mix together lemonade, brandy, and beer; add ice cubes and stir vigorously. Let stand a few minutes and serve. Serves 4.

A "Kulminator" is not the first cousin to the well-known "Terminator" but a beer from Kulmbach, Germany, which is one of the strongest beers with an alcoholic content of 13.2 percent. A "Kulminator" and the "Terminator" may have something in common— strength.

"My people must drink beer!" This was the proclamation of Frederick the Great of Prussia when he became upset with his people drinking coffee.

21

BEER NOG

4 cups beer
1 cinnamon stick
6 whole cloves
6 egg yolks
1/3 cup sugar

In saucepan, combine beer, cinnamon, and cloves. Cover and bring to a boil. Remove spices from liquid. Cream eggs and sugar together and add slowly to hot beer, beating constantly to prevent curdling. Continue beating until frothy and foamy. Serves 4.

Americans prefer a chilled beer; however, in Europe, more often beer is served at room temperature.

22

BREADS

23-38

BEER DINNER ROLLS

1 1/4-ounce package dry
  yeast
1 cup warm water
  (105-115 degrees)
2 tablespoons sugar
1 egg, slightly beaten
2/3 cup milk
1 teaspoon salt
6-8 tablespoons butter or
  margarine, melted,
  divided
4-5 cups flour
1/2 cup beer, room temperature

Dissolve yeast in warm water in large bowl and add sugar, egg, milk, salt, and 2 tablespoons butter. Gradually add small amount of flour to mixture, alternating with small amounts of beer. Mix thoroughly after each addition. When dough is slightly moist, knead until bubbles appear. Cover all sides of dough with remaining butter. Cover dough with towel and let rise in a warm place for approximately 1-1 1/2 hours.

Form rolls of desired shape (cloverleaf, parkerhouse, butterfly, fan-tan, etc.) and let rise in warm place for 1-1 1/2 hours.

Bake in 475-degree oven until brown. They bake quickly, 12-15 minutes. Makes 30-36 rolls.

Most beer-drinking women tend to be in their mid-twenties and under the age of 60 years.

24

BUTTERMILK BEER BREAD (BBB)

3 ounces dry yeast
1½ cups warm water
  (105-115 degrees)
½ cup brown sugar, packed
2 teaspoons salt
¾ cup buttermilk
1 cup beer
6-6½ cups all-purpose white
  flour, divided
3 cups rye flour
¼ cup cooking oil
1 tablespoon caraway seed
  (optional)
4 tablespoons butter,
  melted

In large mixing bowl, dissolve yeast in water, sugar, and salt. Add buttermilk, beer, and 3 cups white flour and mix well. Add rye flour, oil, and caraway seeds and mix well. Add additional white flour to make a stiff dough and knead until smooth and elastic. Put in greased bowl, turning dough so as to cover all sides. Cover with towel and let rise to doubled in bulk in a draft-free place. Remove bread to lightly floured surface and knead again; place in bowl and let rise to doubled in bulk. Cut in 4 equal portions and put in greased loaf pans. Let rise in warm place until doubled in size.

Bake in 375-degree oven for 40-45 minutes or until loaves sound hollow when tapped. Brush with melted butter. Makes 4 loaves.

Beer was an influential factor in the economics of medieval Europe; it was used for trading, taxing, tithing, and payment.

25

OAT BRAN BEER BREAD

3/4 cup beer
2 tablespoons butter or
   margarine
1 13-ounce package
   hot roll mix
1 egg
1/2 cup oat bran
2 tablespoons sugar

In saucepan or in microwave, heat beer and butter until warm, 105-115 degrees. Pour into mixing bowl; add yeast packet from roll mix and dissolve. Add rest of ingredients including flour from roll mix and blend well. Place in greased bowl, cover, and let rise to doubled in size. Punch down; knead and shape into loaf and place in greased loaf pan. Cover and let rise for 35 minutes. Bake at 350 degrees for 40-45 minutes. Makes 1 loaf.

Many of the herbs and seasonings of today were not known to early Americans, so beer was often added to give stews and soups flavor.

"Breweriana" is the name given to the beer memorabilia that a collector accumulates.

TWO-FLOUR MUSTARD BREAD

4   1-ounce packages dry
    yeast
1   12-ounce can warm beer
    (105-115 degrees)
4   teaspoons brown sugar
3½-4 cups white flour
½   cup Dijon mustard
½   cup butter or
    margarine, melted
1   teaspoon salt
1½-2 cups whole wheat flour
    Vegetable cooking spray

Dissolve yeast in warm beer in large bowl; let stand 5 minutes. Add sugar and 3½ cups white flour and beat at low speed of an electric mixer until smooth. Cover and let rise in draft-free place for 30-40 minutes until light and bubbly.

Stir in mustard, melted butter, and salt. Gradually add small amounts of whole wheat flour, stirring well to form soft dough. On a lightly floured surface, knead dough until smooth. Spray large bowl with vegetable spray and turn dough in bowl to cover all sides; cover with towel and let rise in warm place until doubled in size.

Punch down. Put on floured surface and knead until smooth and elastic. Divide dough into two loaves and place in oil-sprayed loaf pans; cover and let rise until doubled in size. Bake at 375 degrees for 30-40 minutes; remove from pan and cool. Makes 2 loaves.

27

SWEDISH BEER BREAD

2 cups beer
2/3 cup molasses
1 1/2 cups warm water
    (105-115 degrees)
1 1/4-ounce package dry
    yeast
5 cups rye flour
1 teaspoon salt
5 cups all-purpose flour
4 tablespoons butter, melted

In large bowl, combine beer, molasses, water, and yeast; let stand 10-12 minutes. Add rye flour and salt. Blend well and add all-purpose flour to form stiff dough. Knead until smooth and elastic. In lightly greased bowl, place dough and turn to cover all sides. Cover and let rise in draft-free place until doubled in bulk, about 2 hours. Divide into 4 portions and shape into round loaves. Place loaves on greased cookie sheets and cover; let rise until doubled in bulk. Bake in 400-degree oven for 12-15 minutes; reduce heat to 350 degrees and bake an additional 25 minutes or until loaves sound hollow when tapped. Brush with melted butter. Cool on racks before slicing. Makes 4 loaves.

Stout is a dark, sweet beer that is made from roasted malt and hops and fermented at warm temperatures (over 60 degrees Fahrenheit).

OLD COUNTRY BEER BREAD

½ cup warm water
(105-115 degrees)
2 1-ounce packages dry
yeast
2 cups beer
⅔ cup molasses
⅓ cup butter, melted
Rind of 1 orange, grated
1½ teaspoons anise
½ teaspoon salt
4 cups rye flour
4 cups white flour

Glaze:
2 tablespoons molasses
2 tablespoons water

Put warm water into large mixing bowl and sprinkle with yeast; stir until dissolved. Add all other ingredients except white flour; beat until smooth. Add white flour to make stiff dough. Knead on lightly floured board until smooth. Cover with cloth and let rise in warm place until twice original size, about 1 hour. Punch down and put on floured board. Divide dough into 2 equal sections; shape each into round ball and flatten on top and bottom to approximately 6-8 inches in diameter. Place on greased baking sheet, cover and let rise again until doubled in size. Prick tops of loaves five or six times with a fork. Bake in preheated oven at 325 degrees for 25 minutes.

Combine molasses and water to make glaze. Remove bread from oven and quickly brush loaves with half of glaze mixture; return loaves to oven for an additional 12-15 minutes. Take out of oven and brush with remaining glaze. Let cool and dry before slicing. Makes 2 loaves.

GERMAN BEER BREAD

1	12-ounce can beer
1/2	cup dark molasses
1/2	cup dark corn syrup
1/2	cup butter
1	cup currants
3	cups cake flour
1/2	teaspoon baking soda
1	teaspoon baking powder
1	teaspoon salt
1	teaspoon cinnamon
1/4	teaspoon nutmeg
1/2	cup chopped nuts

In a saucepan, combine beer, molasses, corn syrup, and butter. Bring to a boil and add currants. Allow mixture to cool. Sift dry ingredients together and gradually stir into the beer mixture. Add chopped nuts. Pour batter into a well-greased 9 x 13-inch cake pan. Bake in a 350-degree oven for 40-45 minutes. Top with icing, if desired. Serves 12-16.

The colloquialism, "a dog's nose" refers to a beer mixed with gin.

Kraeusening is the process of mixing young (newly brewed) beer and aged beer; this creates a natural increase in effervescence. When you drink a brew advertised as "kraeusened," expect more bubbles.

30

PUB BREAD

3 cups self-rising flour
2 tablespoons sugar
1 12-ounce can beer,
     room temperature
4 tablespoons butter, melted

Mix all ingredients except melted butter. Pour into well-greased pan. Bake at 350 degrees for 45 minutes. Remove from oven, pour melted butter over the bread, and return to oven for an additional 10 minutes. Makes 1 loaf.

Wooden barrels that were originally used to store beer were lined with pitch, which prevented the beer from taking on a woody flavor. Today, aluminum and stainless steel kegs are used.

The National Prohibition Act in the years 1920-1933, prohibiting the sale of alcoholic beverages, is reputed to have cost the United States government $34,565,109,245.00 in lost taxes. Some economists refer to this as the "noble experiment."

31

ORANGE BEER BREAD

4 large oranges
1 12-ounce can beer, divided
1/2 teaspoon baking soda
1 1/2 cups sugar
2 1/2 cups all-purpose white flour
1/2 teaspoon salt
3 teaspoons baking powder
1/2 cup walnuts, chopped
2 eggs, beaten
2 tablespoons butter or margarine, melted

Wash oranges and, with a sharp knife, peel off thin layer of orange rind (do not get any of the bitter white membrane). Cut rind into small pieces and put in saucepan; cover with 1 cup beer. Reserve remaining 1/2 cup beer. Add soda to orange rind and beer mixture and bring to boil. Cook for 15 minutes. Drain and rinse orange rind with cold water.

Return orange rind to pan and add sugar; cook slowly until rind is candied and transparent, about 15 minutes. Mixture will be syrupy.

Sift flour, salt, and baking powder into large mixing bowl. Add nuts and stir. In separate bowl, combine eggs and reserved 1/2 cup beer; stir into flour mixture. Stir in melted butter and orange rind mixture. Blend well—dough will be stiff. Spoon into greased and floured loaf pan and bake at 300 degrees for 1 hour. Makes 1 loaf.

32

DATE AND NUT BREAD

2½ cups flour, sifted
4 teaspoons baking powder
½ cup brown sugar
½ cup white sugar
6 tablespoons butter or margarine, softened
1 cup beer, room temperature
1 egg
¾ cup nuts, chopped
1 cup dates, chopped (If cutting dates with kitchen scissors, dip blades in hot water first)

Combine dry ingredients. Cut in butter or margarine with pastry blender or knife to size of rice grains. Add beer and egg and mix just enough to moisten. Add nuts and dates. Put in well-greased and floured loaf pan and bake at 350 degrees for approximately 50 minutes or until a cake tester inserted into bread comes out clean. Cool before slicing. Makes 1 loaf.

"To take a spell" is interpreted in Charles Dickens' David Copperfield *to mean a stop at a local tavern for a beer.*

To the people of the ancient world, beer was more than just a beverage to consume. The Babylonians appointed goddesses to watch over their beer, and the Egyptians offered it as a gift to their gods.

MICROWAVE BREAD

1 tablespoon yellow cornmeal
2 cups all-purpose flour
1 cup whole wheat flour
1 1-ounce envelope onion
  soup mix, divided
3 tablespoons sugar
2 teaspoons baking powder
1 12-ounce can beer
1 tablespoon butter or
  margarine

Lightly coat 9 x 5-inch microwave-safe loaf pan with vegetable cooking spray. Sprinkle bottom and sides with cornmeal. Mix flours, 1/4 cup soup mix, sugar, and baking powder in large bowl. Add beer and stir until well blended. Spread batter in loaf pan and dot with butter; sprinkle with remaining soup mix.

Place pan in microwave oven on oven trivet or inverted saucer. Microwave uncovered on medium heat 9-12 minutes, rotating pan twice, until pick inserted in center comes out clean (moist spots on top will dry while it cools). Place pan directly on heat-proof surface for 10 minutes; remove to rack. Serve hot or at room temperature. Makes 1 loaf.

If you prefer not to have a "collar" or "head" on your glass of beer, tilt the glass and pour the beer down the side.

BEER AND CHEESE MUFFINS

3 cups flour
5 teaspoons baking powder
1/2 teaspoon salt
1 tablespoon sugar
1 12-ounce can beer
4 tablespoons butter, melted
1 cup coarsely grated cheddar
   cheese

Combine flour, baking powder, salt, and sugar in bowl and pour in beer, stirring to blend.

Fill greased muffin pans 3/4 full. Brush with melted butter and sprinkle with cheese. Bake at 375 degrees for 15-20 minutes, until browned. Makes 24 muffins.

"Brewer's yeast," a by-product of the fermentation process in the brewing of beer, is advocated by some health people as a source of protein and vitamin B.

35

BISQUICK AND BEER MUFFINS

2 cups Bisquick
1 cup shredded cheddar cheese
2 tablespoons sugar
1 cup beer

Combine Bisquick, cheese, and sugar and blend in beer. Fill greased muffin tins 2/3 full; let stand 15 minutes before baking. Bake in 375-degree oven for 15 minutes. Makes 12 muffins.

By law, beer in Colonial America had to be served in standard half-pint, pint, or quart vessels. When tin could no longer be imported from England, American pewter production stopped. It then became fashionable to melt down and recast old pewter mugs from England.

BEER CROUTONS

1 loaf day-old bread
1 12-ounce can cold beer
1/2 - 3/4 cup grated Parmesan
    cheese

Remove and discard crust from bread; cut bread into half-inch cubes. Dip cubes of bread into cold beer, then roll in grated cheese. Place on a buttered baking sheet and bake at 450 degrees for 10-12 minutes, until golden brown. Use as snack food or serve with soup or salad. Makes 6 cups.

In Egypt, 1600 B.C., everyone consumed beer. The wealthy sipped their beer through golden straws in private brewhouses while the common folk drank at local taverns.

37

BUTTERMILK BEER PANCAKES

3 eggs
3/4 cup buttermilk
3/4 cup beer
1 teaspoon salt
1 cup flour
1/4 cup granola
2 tablespoons peanut oil

Put eggs, buttermilk, and beer in a food blender; blend until combined. Add salt, flour, and granola; blend until bubbly. Scrape down side of blender and blend until mixture is smooth, about 2 minutes total in blender.

Heat peanut oil in griddle or skillet until hot. Spoon batter on griddle in dollops. When top side begins to bubble, turn pancake and cook until lightly browned. Makes 16.

Excise tax is a surcharge placed on the manufacture, sale, or consumption of beer.

38

SALADS & SIDE DISHES

39-52

BEERY BEAN SALAD

1   16-ounce can small green
    peas
1   16-ounce can French cut
    green beans
1   cup diced celery
½   cup diced red onion
½   cup salad oil
½   cup beer
½   cup vinegar
1   cup sugar
    Worcestershire sauce to
      taste
    Salt and pepper to taste

Drain juice from peas and beans; add celery and onion to vegetables. Stir in salad oil to coat. In small saucepan, mix beer, vinegar, and sugar and bring to boil. Remove from heat and cool. Add Worcestershire sauce and seasonings to taste and pour over vegetable mixture. Serves 6-8.

The "Courtship of Miles Standish" tells of the marriage of John Alden to Prisilla, but it doesn't say he was the cooper in charge of the beer barrels during the voyage of the Mayflower. He originally planned to return to his home in Essex, England.

KARTOFFEL SALADE
(German Potato Salad)

7-8 potatoes, boiled, peeled, sliced, cooled

1½ cups chopped onion

¾ cup diced bacon

¾ cup vinegar

¾ cup flour

1 12-ounce can beer

¾ cup sugar

2 tablespoons salt

¾ cup water

Sprinkle cold potatoes with chopped onions; cover and let stand in refrigerator overnight, if possible.

In a large skillet, fry bacon to a golden brown; add vinegar and heat to boiling. Blend flour and beer in separate bowl to make a paste; add to boiling mixture. Add sugar, salt, and water to mixture and boil for approximately 5 minutes longer.

Pour hot dressing over potatoes and onions, mixing well. Let stand in warm oven (200 degrees or less) for about 2-3 hours to allow flavors to blend. Serves 6.

During the time of the Crusades, beer was a very common drink because the quality of the water was questionable; the brewing process produced a safer drinking product.

† BEER LIME SALAD

1 cup beer
1 cup water
1 6-ounce package lime
    flavored gelatin
1 20-ounce can crushed
    pineapple
1 cup diced celery
1 cup sour half-and-half

Mix beer and water together in saucepan and bring to boil. Pour liquids in bowl with gelatin, stirring to dissolve gelatin. Add pineapple with juice and celery, mixing well. Chill in refrigerator until thickened. Add sour half-and-half and put in 1½-quart mold. Chill until firm. Serves 6.

Beer enjoys the distinction of having been transported to North America on the Mayflower. A journal entry dated December 19, 1620 by one of the Mayflower's passengers, indicates, "...we could not now take time for further search or consideration, our victuals being much spent, especially our beere."

BEER BAKED BEANS

1   32-ounce can baked beans
1   cup beer
1/2 cup brewed coffee
1/2 cup chopped tomato
3/4 cup chopped onion
3   frankfurters, cut in 1-inch diagonal pieces
1   tablespoon horseradish
1/2 cup ketchup
1/2 cup molasses

P lace all ingredients in oven-proof dish and mix well. Bake at 325 degrees until hot, approximately 1 hour, stirring occasionally. If beans appear to be drying out, add small amount of additional beer. Serves 6-8.

Talk about fringe benefits: "beer money" was an allowance of a penny a day given to non-commissioned officers and soldiers in the British Army between 1800 and 1873 in place of an issue of beer or spirits.

CHUCK WAGON BEER BEANS

3 cups navy beans
1 pound salt pork
3 12-ounce cans beer
3/4 cup dark molasses
2 teaspoons dry mustard
1/2 cup grated onions
1/4 teaspoon paprika

Place beans in a pot, cover with cold water and let soak overnight. The beans will absorb the water; drain off any remaining water. Cover with fresh water and cook with cover on for 1 hour. Drain water from beans and reserve.

In heavy casserole, put 1/2 of salt pork on the bottom; place beans on top. Blend beer, molasses, dry mustard, onions, and paprika; pour over beans. Lift beans carefully with a spoon so juice penetrates to the bottom of the casserole. Add sufficient reserved bean water to barely cover beans. Place remaining salt pork on top. Cover the casserole and bake in 300-degree oven for approximately 6 hours. Once each hour, add a little reserved bean water if necessary to keep beans slightly covered with liquid. If there is not sufficient liquid, beans can become dry and hard. Remove the cover from the casserole for the last hour of baking. Serves 8.

SWEET AND SOUR GREEN BEANS

1 pound green beans (frozen
   or canned green beans
   may be substituted for
   fresh beans)
3/4 teaspoon salt, divided
4 slices bacon, cut into
   1-inch pieces
1/3 cup diced onion
2/3 cup beer
2 tablespoons brown sugar

Wash and snap off ends of beans. Put beans into saucepan; cover with water and 1/2 teaspoon salt. Bring to boil and continue to boil approximately 15-20 minutes, until beans are tender. (If using frozen or canned beans, follow directions for cooking on package or container.)

Fry bacon in skillet until lightly browned. Add onions, beer, brown sugar, and remaining salt; bring to boil. Pour bacon mixture over drained green beans and toss lightly to mix. Serves 4.

The United States leads in the production of beer, followed by Germany in second place, and England in third.

CHEESE SAUCE OVER ASPARAGUS

2-3 pounds fresh asparagus
1 tablespoon butter
1 pound sharp cheddar cheese, shredded
3/4 cup beer
1 egg yolk, lightly beaten
1/2 teaspoon Worcestershire sauce
1/2 teaspoon dry mustard
1/2 teaspoon Tabasco sauce
Salt and white pepper to taste
Paprika for garnish

Steam or gently boil asparagus until tender; set aside.

In top of double boiler, melt butter and cheese; gradually stir in beer as cheese begins to melt. Add some hot cheese mixture to beaten egg yolk, blending well; then add all of egg mixture to cheese sauce. Stir in Worcestershire sauce, dry mustard, Tabasco sauce, salt, and pepper. Continue cooking and stirring until sauce is thickened and smooth. Pour over asparagus and garnish with paprika.

If there is left-over sauce, add a little beer and mix with mixer until smooth. Reheat in saucepan over medium heat. Serves 8.

A 12-ounce bottle of a soft drink and a 12-ounce bottle of beer have equivalent calories—about 150—but beer has more nutritional value than soda.

CROCKED CARROTS

1   pound baby carrots
1   tablespoon butter
1   cup beer
1/4 teaspoon salt
1   teaspoon brown sugar

Rinse and cut baby carrots into quarters. In skillet, melt butter; add beer and carrots. Cook over low heat until tender, stirring often. Stir in salt and sugar. Cook for an additional 2-3 minutes. Serve hot. Serves 4-5.

Shakespeare enjoyed his mug of beer to the extent that he used the drink as part of his play action on many occasions; i.e. "I shall make it a felony to drink small beer," in King Henry VI.

In the year 812, Charlemagne listed in his Capitulare De Villis Imperialibus *the fact that beer brewers were public administrators.*

SAUTEED KALE

2 pounds fresh kale
2 tablespoons butter or
    margarine
1½ cups sliced onions
¾ cup diced red or green
    pepper
2 cloves garlic, crushed
½ cup diced baked ham
¼ teaspoon Tabasco sauce
½ cup beer
2 teaspoons vinegar

Cut off and discard kale stems. Trim off tough center rib that runs up the leaf and discard. Rinse leaves well and cut into 1-inch pieces.

In large skillet over medium-high heat, melt butter or margarine; add onions, pepper, and garlic. Saute until onions are tender. Add kale, ham, and Tabasco sauce; saute until well coated. Add beer; cover and reduce heat. Simmer until kale is tender, 20-25 minutes, stirring occasionally. Stir in vinegar and serve. Serves 6.

The "official" credit for the use of hops in making beer is generally given to Abbess Hildegard of Rupertsburg at around 1079; however, there were public records indicating its use two hundred years earlier.

BREWED SAUERKRAUT

3 strips bacon, diced
1 cup chopped onion
2 pounds sauerkraut, rinsed
and drained
1 12-ounce can beer
2 tablespoons brown sugar,
packed
1/2 teaspoon caraway seeds
Pepper to taste
1 cup coarsely shredded
carrot

Fry bacon in 2-quart saucepan until crisp. Remove, drain, and set aside. Add onions to pan and saute; stir in sauerkraut, beer, sugar, caraway seeds, and pepper. Bring to a boil, cover, and simmer for 1 hour. Add carrots and simmer uncovered for an additional 20 minutes, until carrots are tender. Spoon into serving bowl and garnish with bacon pieces. Serves 6.

Thomas Jefferson, third president of the United States, brewed beer at his Monticello home in Virginia. He wrote, "I wish to see this beverage (beer) become common instead of whiskey which kills one-third of our citizens and ruins their families."

49

✝ POTATO PANCAKES

5-6 large baking potatoes
1 cup diced onion
3 eggs, lightly beaten
3/4 cup beer
4 tablespoons flour
2 teaspoons salt
White pepper to taste
4-6 tablespoons margarine or butter
Sour cream

Peel and grate potatoes; place potatoes in strainer over a bowl, pressing potatoes to release all liquid. Drain for a few minutes, reserving liquid. Place potatoes and foamy opaque portion of reserved liquid into bowl. Add onion to potatoes; mix well. Stir in eggs, beer, flour, salt, and pepper.

In skillet, melt butter and when it is very hot, spoon 1/2 cup potato mixture into skillet and fry on both sides until golden brown. Remove from skillet and drain on paper towel. Keep warm and continue making pancakes until all batter is used. Serve with dollops of sour cream.

Instead of sour cream, these can be served with melted butter mixed with chopped onions or with an applesauce topping, too. Serves 6.

Beer was a popular drink among the Roman soldiers.
In medieval Europe, beer was brewed by the monks.

CAULIFLOWER TEMPURA

4 cups vegetable oil
2 cups beer
2½ cups flour, divided
1 teaspoon salt
2 teaspoons sweet paprika
1 head cauliflower, trimmed,
   washed and cut into
   florets

Put oil into deep fryer and heat to 375 degrees.

Mix beer, 2 cups flour, salt, and paprika in food mixer and blend until smooth. Pour into shallow bowl.

Dip cauliflower pieces into remaining flour and then into batter. Place in hot oil, a few at a time, for 3-4 minutes until golden brown. Drain on paper towel and serve hot. Serve with mustard sauce, if desired. Serves 6-8.

Today, dried fruits and vegetables are staples for a backpacking trip, but in ancient Egypt, malt was baked into flat cakes and carried by the soldiers who used them to brew an instant beer.

DEEP FRIED BROCCOLI

2-3 pounds broccoli, washed, trimmed, cut into florets
2 teaspoons salt, divided
1 tablespoon sugar
1 1/2 cups flour
4 cups plus 1 teaspoon vegetable oil, divided
1/2 cup beer
2 eggs, separated

Cook broccoli in boiling water with 1 teaspoon salt and sugar for 15 minutes until tender. Drain and set aside.

Mix flour, remaining 1 teaspoon salt, 1 teaspoon oil, and beer in mixing bowl. Add lightly beaten egg yolks to batter; cover and let stand at room temperature for 1 hour. Just before using, beat egg whites until stiff and fold into batter. Heat 4 cups oil in deep fryer to 360 degrees. Dip broccoli pieces into batter and fry in hot oil until crisp and lightly browned, 3-4 minutes. Serves 6-8.

In the 1880's, a well-known baseball player, Mike Kelly, was criticized by Sporting News *for holding up a game because he stopped for a drink of beer.*

52

SOUPS & STEWS

53-78

BREAD AND BEER SOUP

2 cups beef bouillon
4 slices rye bread
2 cups beer
2 tablespoons sugar
1/2 tablespoon grated lemon
   rind
1/2 teaspoon cinnamon
1/4 teaspoon nutmeg
1 cup sour cream

Pour bouillon in large saucepan and add bread slices. As bread softens, break in smaller pieces with wooden spoon. Add beer, sugar, and spices; bring to a boil. Taste and adjust seasonings as desired. Serve hot with a dollop of sour cream on each bowl. Serves 4.

Because almost all beer wholesalers, distributors, and retailers are independently owned and operated, there is no monopoly. The competition is there and the consumer has a choice.

54

SPLIT PEA SOUP

1 pound split green peas, rinsed
2 12-ounce cans beer
6 cups water
1 cup shredded carrots
1 cup diced celery
8 tablespoons dried onion flakes
1 meaty smoked ham bone, fat trimmed off
½ teaspoon salt
½ teaspoon ground black pepper
Seasoned croutons, garnish

In heavy kettle, combine peas, beer, water, carrots, celery, onion flakes, ham bone, salt, and pepper. Heat to boiling, stirring frequently. Reduce heat and simmer until peas have cooked down to a soup-like texture, about 1 hour. Remove ham bone and remove meat from bone. Return meat to soup; discard bone and any fat accumulation. Return to heat, stirring occasionally, for approximately 30 minutes. Serve hot, garnished with seasoned croutons. May be frozen. Serves 8.

During the Revolutionary War, George Washington made sure his troops received a quart of beer each day.

55

Very good
Node ~
Jov. 98

TANGY TOMATO CONSOMME

2 10½-ounce cans beef broth
1 12-ounce can beer
4 cups tomato juice
6 whole cloves
1 bunch celery, tops and
   leaves, diced
1 teaspoon celery salt
2 teaspoons sugar
1 tablespoon lemon juice
1 medium onion, thinly sliced

In large saucepan, mix all ingredients. Bring to boil, then reduce heat and simmer for approximately 20-25 minutes. Strain and serve. Serves 7-8.

In 1637, the legislature of the Massachusetts Bay Colony met to fix the price of beer. After lengthy deliberation, the new price was announced: "Not more than one penny a quart at the most."

56

EASY BEER ONION SOUP

1/4 cup butter
1   pound yellow onions, sliced
     finely and rings cut in half
2   tablespoons flour
1/2 teaspoon salt
1   10 1/2-ounce can beef broth
1   10 1/2-ounce can chicken
     broth
1   12-ounce can beer
6   thin slices French bread
6   slices mozzarella cheese
     (1/2 cup Parmesan cheese
     may be substituted)

Melt butter in heavy saucepan. Add onions, flour, and salt; cook for 15 minutes until golden brown. Add beef broth, chicken broth, and beer. Cover tightly and reduce heat; simmer for 15-20 minutes.

Toast bread until golden brown and place 1 slice at bottom of each of 6 serving dishes. Ladle soup over bread and top with cheese. If using mozzarella cheese, put under broiler for a few minutes to melt. Serves 6-8.

In May 1904 the Ladies Home Journal *contained the quote: "A mother who would hold up her hands in holy horror at the thought of her child drinking a glass of beer, which contains from 2 to 5 per cent alcohol, gives to that child with her own hands a potent medicine that contains from 17 to 44 per cent alcohol." Check the alcohol content of some well-known cough syrups.*

MOM'S ONION SOUP

2 tablespoons butter
2 pounds onions, sliced
4 cups beef stock
4 cups chicken stock
1 12-ounce can beer
1 clove fresh garlic, minced
1/8 teaspoon salt
1/8 teaspoon white pepper
1 1/2 cups croutons
6-8 slices mozzarella cheese

Melt butter in heavy saucepan and saute onions until golden. Add beef stock, chicken stock, beer, garlic, salt, and pepper; bring to boil. Reduce heat and simmer for 15-20 minutes.

Place croutons at bottom of individual bowls; ladle soup on top. Cover each with slice of mozzarella cheese. Place in broiler until cheese becomes bubbly. Serves 6-8.

St. Gambrinus, according to Webster's abridged dictionary, is a mythical Flemish king who is said to be the inventor of beer; credit for inventing beer is also given to the Egyptian god Osiris. It is not really important who did it; what is important is that somebody did it!

VEGETABLE-BEER-CHEESE SOUP

2 12-ounce cans beer
4 cubes chicken bouillon
3 cups shredded potatoes
2 cups finely chopped onicns
1/2 cup shredded carrots
1/2 cup finely chopped celery
1/2 pound cheddar cheese,
    shredded
1 cup half-and-half
1/8 teaspoon ground nutmeg
1/4 cup minced parsley,
    garnish

In large saucepan, mix beer and bouillon and bring to boil. Add vegetables; return to boiling point. Reduce heat, cover, and simmer about 15 minutes. Add cheese, half-and-half, and nutmeg. Heat thoroughly.

Serve garnished with parsley. Serves 7-8.

Married women consume more beer than their single counterparts; is it the desire to share with their husbands or cultivated taste buds?

WISCONSIN CHEESE SOUP

4	cups milk
1	cup chicken broth
2/3	cup beer
1	tablespoon butter
1/2	cup diced green peppers
1/2	cup diced carrots
1/4	cup diced celery
1/4	cup diced onion
3/4	cup flour
1 1/2	cups grated cheese

Mix milk, chicken broth, and beer in saucepan over medium heat. Melt butter in skillet and saute peppers, carrots, celery, and onion. Add to heated liquids. Blend in flour and cheese until melted, approximately 5-7 minutes. Serves 6.

Sundowner is a South African expression for the first glass of beer after the sun has set.

JOHN'S BEER CHEESE SOUP

½ cup butter
1 cup shredded carrots
½ cup diced celery
½ cup diced onion
5 cups chicken broth
1 12-ounce can flat beer,
     room temperature
½ cup flour
½ teaspoon dry mustard
1 tablespoon grated
     Parmesan cheese
½ pound sharp cheddar cheese,
     grated
Salt and white pepper to
     taste
Minced parsley, garnish

In large saucepan, melt butter. Add carrots, celery, and onion and saute. Add chicken broth and beer; heat to simmer until vegetables are cooked. Add flour, dry mustard, and Parmesan cheese and continue cooking at low to medium heat until mixture thickens, 5-7 minutes. Add grated cheddar cheese and seasonings. Cook until cheese is melted and vegetables are cooked, 5-7 minutes. Serve garnished with minced parsley. Serves 6-8.

Bock beer was first brewed in the German city of Einbeck and confused by some to sound like "ein Bock" meaning "male goat."

61

FRANKFURTER SOUP

1   **pound dried navy beans**
7   **cups water**
2   **cups beef broth**
2   **cups beer**
1   **carrot, grated**
1/2   **cup chopped celery**
4   **strips bacon, diced**
3/4   **cup diced onions**
1/2   **teaspoon salt**
1/4   **teaspoon white pepper**
7-8   **frankfurters,**
     sliced at angle
2   **tablespoons chopped**
     parsley, garnish

In large saucepan, soak beans in water overnight.

Add beef broth and beer to beans and water and bring to a boil. Continue to cook for approximately 1 hour. Add carrots and celery and cook an additional 30 minutes.

In skillet, fry bacon until golden brown. Add onions and saute until transparent. Set aside.

Drain bean mixture, reserving liquid. In sieve or food mill, mash bean mixture, forming a rather thick texture. (If you prefer to just mash the soup mixture with potato masher, you can do so.) Return to pan with liquid and add onion/bacon mixture. Add seasonings and frankfurters and heat. Sprinkle servings with chopped parsley. Serves 5-6.

Corks are commonly used to seal wine bottles, but did you know that up until the 1890's beer bottles were also sealed with corks?

TURKEY AND BEER SOUP

4 tablespoons butter or margarine
1 pound skinless ground turkey
1/2 cup chopped onion
1 12-ounce can beer
1 10½-ounce can chicken broth
1½ cups water
1½ cups thinly sliced carrots
1 cup grated turnip
1/2 cup sliced celery
1 4-ounce can mushroom pieces with juice
1 bay leaf
1/2 teaspoon salt
1/8 teaspoon pepper
1/4 teaspoon ground nutmeg

Melt butter in large saucepan and brown turkey and onion. Add beer, broth, water, vegetables, bay leaf, and seasonings. Bring to boil; reduce heat. Cover and simmer for 40 minutes, until vegetables are tender. Remove bay leaf before serving. Serves 5.

The hinged top of a beer stein is the result of a 16th century German law that decreed all food and drinking vessels should have lids because of the swarms of insects which plagued the country.

63

+ TURKEY CHILI

2 pounds ground, skinless turkey
3 large onions, chopped
1 cup chopped celery
2 cups chopped green pepper
1 28-ounce can peeled tomatoes
2 6-ounce cans tomato paste
1 12-ounce can beer
2 tablespoons chili powder
2 tablespoons cumin
2 16-ounce cans chili pinto beans
1 16-ounce can red kidney beans
Chopped raw onions and grated cheese, garnish

In large saucepan, brown turkey meat with onions and celery, adding small amount vegetable oil if necessary so meat does not stick to pan. Add peppers, tomatoes, tomato paste, beer, and spices, blending well. Add beans and simmer an additional 20-30 minutes.

Serve with chopped raw onions and grated cheese on top. Serves 10-12.

Good Queen Bess of England may be criticized for ordering the beheading of Mary, Queen of Scots, but when Queen Mary demanded her own supply of beer during her imprisonment, Bess did grant the request.

CHILI SOUP

4 tablespoons vegetable oil, divided

4 cups chopped onion

2 pounds lean pork shoulder, diced

1 pound lean ground beef

4 cloves garlic, minced

5 tablespoons chili powder

1 tablespoon cumin

2 14-16-ounce cans tomatoes, chopped

1 10 1/2-ounce can beef broth

1 12-ounce can beer

1 tablespoon dried coriander

2 teaspoons oregano

1 4-ounce can green chilies, chopped

2 16-ounce cans dark red kidney beans, drained

1 teaspoon salt (optional)
   Green onions and shredded cheese, garnish

In Dutch oven, heat 3 tablespoons oil; add onions and saute until lightly browned. Remove onions with slotted spoon and set aside.

Add remaining tablespoon oil to Dutch oven; add meats and brown. Pour off fat; add garlic, chili powder, and cumin. Cook, stirring frequently, for 2 minutes. Add tomatoes, broth, beer, coriander, oregano, chilies, and reserved onions. Reduce heat and simmer covered for 3 hours, stirring occasionally. Add beans and salt, if desired. Cook an additional 15 minutes. Serve with green onions and shredded cheese as garnishes. Serves 12-15.

It has been reported that a combination of beer and dish soap in an open pan will discourage wasps from forming nests in your backyard.

✝ CHILI

3 tablespoons vegetable oil
1 cup diced green pepper
1 cup diced onion
1/2 cup diced celery
3 pounds ground chuck
1 12-ounce can beer
1 10-ounce can tomato sauce
8 tablespoons onion flakes
5 tablespoons chili powder
1 tablespoon ground cumin
1 teaspoon salt
1/8 teaspoon ground red pepper
1 bay leaf

Heat oil in large saucepan until hot; saute pepper, onion, and celery. Add beef and cook until browned, stirring to keep in small pieces. Add beer, tomato sauce, onion flakes, chili powder, cumin, salt, red pepper, and bay leaf. Bring to a boil, then reduce heat and simmer for approximately 2 hours. Before serving remove bay leaf. This is a good, hearty, thick chili. Makes 12-15 servings.

It is said that doctors in Einbeck, Germany, prescribed two glasses of dark beer before bedtime for insomniacs.

CARBONNADE OF BEEF

1/4 cup flour
1 teaspoon salt
1/8 teaspoon pepper
3 pounds stew beef, cut into
    1-inch cubes
1/4 pound bacon, cut into
    1-inch pieces
4 cups diced onions
2 cloves garlic, chopped
1 tablespoon brown sugar
1 12-ounce can beer
1 cup beef broth
1 bay leaf
1/2 teaspoon thyme

Mix flour, salt, and pepper in bag; add beef and shake to coat on all sides. In Dutch oven, cook bacon until crisp. Remove with slotted spoon and drain on paper towel. To bacon drippings, add beef a few pieces at a time and brown. As beef cubes are browned, remove and set aside. Add onions and garlic and saute until translucent, about 5 minutes. Add brown sugar and cook an additional 5 minutes. Return beef and bacon to pan and add remaining ingredients. Cover and simmer over low heat for about 1 1/2 hours. Uncover and continue to simmer for an additional 30 minutes, until juices concentrate to desired consistency and meat is tender. Remove bay leaf before serving. Serves 10-12.

Many glasses of beer have been lifted to "toast" good health without being aware that the origin of this custom came from placing a piece of toasted bread in a wine cup to add nutritive value.

67

BAR-B-CUE BEER STEW

1½ pounds lean flank steak
2 8-ounce cans tomato sauce
1 15-ounce can pinto beans, drained
¾ cup diced celery
1 clove garlic, minced
1 cup flat beer
¼ cup cider vinegar
¼ cup Worcestershire sauce
3 tablespoons brown sugar

Trim all fat from steak; slice meat diagonally across grain into thin slices. (Steak will slice easier if partially frozen.) Place meat slices in large, heavy saucepan and cover with all remaining ingredients. Bring to a boil. Cover, reduce heat, and simmer for 1½-2 hours, until meat is tender. Stir occasionally to avoid mixture sticking to bottom of pan. Serves 4-6.

Long before the time of Confucius, the Chinese brewed with millet, a cereal grain. According to very old sacred books, beer played an important role in early Chinese religious rituals.

BEER BAKED STEW

1 teaspoon salt
1 teaspoon pepper
1 teaspoon paprika
2 pounds lean stew beef
6 medium potatoes
½ cup diced onions
3 carrots, diced
2 tablespoons dry onion
    soup mix
1 10 ¾-ounce can cream of
    celery soup, undiluted
1 12-ounce can beer

Mix salt, pepper, and paprika in a paper bag; place meat in bag and shake meat to cover all sides. Transfer meat to oven-proof casserole and add potatoes, onions, carrots, and onion soup mix. Blend cream of celery soup with beer and pour over meat. Bake covered in 250-300 degree oven for a minimum of 5 hours, until meat is tender. Good served with baking powder biscuits. Serves 8-10.

After beer is fermented and before it has been properly aged, it is referred to as "green beer." Food coloring is sometimes added to beer on St. Patrick's Day and called "green beer," too.

69

✛ PAUL'S BEER STEW

1/4   cup butter or margarine
2   pounds beef chuck, cut
      into 1½-inch cubes
    Salt and pepper to taste
1/8   teaspoon thyme
1   bay leaf
1   tablespoon brown sugar
1   tablespoon vinegar
1   12-ounce can of beer
      (approximately)
6   medium carrots, cut into
      1-inch pieces
6   medium potatoes, cut into
      1½-inch cubes
2   cups diced onions
2   stalks celery, cut into
      1½-inch pieces

In heavy Dutch oven, melt butter or margarine and braise meat cubes. Add salt, pepper, thyme, bay leaf, brown sugar, and vinegar. Add beer to cover. Bring to boil and simmer for 2 hours over low to medium-high heat. Add vegetables to meat and cook an additional 1 hour. Taste and add additional salt and pepper, if desired. Serves 8-10.

Most of the ancient world brewed beer of some kind, but it was the Egyptians and Babylonians who perfected the brewing process.

BEEF CARBONNADE

5 tablespoons vegetable oil, divided

2 pounds boneless chuck, cubed

4 carrots, cut into 1/2-inch slices

2 cups thinly sliced onions

1 clove garlic, minced

1 tablespoon light brown sugar

1/2 cup all-purpose flour

1/2 cup beef broth

1 cup beer

1/3 cup chopped parsley

1 bay leaf

1/2 teaspoon caraway seed (optional)

1/2 teaspoon thyme, crushed

1/4 teaspoon salt

1/4 teaspoon pepper

In large saucepan, heat 2 tablespoons oil over medium-high heat. Add half of meat cubes and cook, turning often, until browned on all sides. With slotted spoon, remove meat from pan and place in 2 1/2-quart casserole or baking dish. Repeat with remaining beef, adding additional tablespoon oil, if necessary.

Preheat oven to 350 degrees. Add carrots, onions, garlic, and brown sugar to saucepan. Cover and cook, stirring occasionally, 10 minutes or until onions are soft. Add remaining 1 tablespoon oil and flour. Cook, stirring in beef broth, beer, parsley, bay leaf, caraway seed, and seasonings. Cook, stirring until thickened, 5-7 minutes. Pour over beef in casserole, cover, and bake 1 hour or more, until beef is tender. Remove bay leaf and discard. Let stand about 15 minutes before serving. Serves 8-10.

BEER STEW

1/2 cup margarine, divided
1 tablespoon salt
1/2 teaspoon pepper
1/2 teaspoon paprika
1/2 cup flour
2 pounds stew beef
1/2 cup diced onions
1/2 cup diced celery stalk and
   leaves
3 tablespoons sugar
2 12-ounce cans beer
5 carrots, cut into 1-inch
   pieces
1 16-ounce package frozen
   green beans
2 bay leaves
1/4 cup finely chopped parsley

Melt 6 tablespoons margarine in heavy skillet. Combine salt, pepper, paprika, and flour in shallow bowl. Dust meat with mixture. Brown meat, onions, and celery in margarine. Remove from pan and place in large casserole. Add remaining 2 tablespoons margarine to skillet and caramelize sugar. Add beer and bring to boil. Pour over meat mixture and put in carrots, beans, and bay leaves. If you like a thicker stew, add some remaining flour mixture. Bake in 350-degree oven for 1 1/2 hours, until bubbly hot. Garnish with parsley. Serves 8-10.

The beer served from the tap in your neighborhood tavern is called draught beer, usually unpasteurized and stored in barrels and kegs. Bottled and canned beer are pasteurized because of their longer "shelf" life.

72

COMPLETE MEAL STEW

3   pounds boneless beef
    chuck, cubed
1/2 cup plus 2 tablespoons
    flour, divided
1/2 teaspoon pepper
4   tablespoons margarine
1/2 cup diced onions
1   10 1/2-ounce can beef broth
1   12-ounce can beer
1   bay leaf
10 small white onions, peeled
6-7 carrots, peeled and cut
    into 1-inch pieces
6   medium potatoes, cut into
    1-inch pieces
2   cups sliced mushrooms
2   tablespoons water

Dust meat in 1/2 cup flour and pepper. Melt margarine in heavy saucepan and saute diced onions. Add meat and brown on all sides. Add broth, beer, and bay leaf. Cover and simmer over low heat for 1 1/2 hours. Add whole onions, carrots, potatoes, and mushrooms. Cover and return to heat until vegetables are tender, approximately 30 minutes. Combine remaining 2 tablespoons flour and water to make paste and add to juices to thicken. Serves 10.

The words of our national anthem, "The Star Spangled Banner," are set to the melody of an old drinking tune, "To Anacreon in Heaven."

73

BEEF STEW

1/2 cup flour
1/4 teaspoon pepper
1 tablespoon salt, divided
1/4 teaspoon paprika
3 pounds beef chuck, trimmed
   and cut into cubes
3 tablespoons butter or
   margarine
1 small onion, diced
3 12-ounce cans beer
1 8-ounce can tomato puree
1 tablespoon brown sugar
1 bay leaf
3 cups chopped celery
3 cups chopped carrots
1 cup frozen peas

Mix flour, pepper, 1 teaspoon salt, and paprika in bag; add meat and shake to coat. In large saucepan, melt butter. Brown meat in butter; remove meat and set aside. Add chopped onions to saucepan and fry until brown.

Return meat to pan. Add beer, remaining salt, tomato puree, brown sugar, and bay leaf; simmer, covered, about 1 1/2 hours, until meat is tender. Remove bay leaf. Add celery and carrots and simmer 15 minutes. Add peas and simmer an additional 15 minutes. Serves 10.

Spruce beer, a favorite in the 17th and 18th centuries, was made in the spring of the year from the fresh shoots of the black and red spruce trees, replacing dried hops.

DAD'S FAVORITE STEW

12 ounces ketchup
1 12-ounce can beer
1/2 cup brown sugar
4 pounds stew beef, cubed
1 cup sliced onion
1/2 teaspoon pepper
1/2 teaspoon garlic powder

Combine ketchup, beer, and brown sugar and blend well. In oven-proof casserole, layer meat, and onions; season with pepper and garlic powder. Pour beer mixture into casserole; cover and bake in 350-degree oven for 3 hours.

If this stew is made the day before serving, the flavor is even better. Serve over potatoes, rice, or noodles. Serves 10-12.

It is reputed that beer was one of the provisions which George Washington requested from Congress when his troops were stationed at Valley Forge.

SPICY BEEF AND BEER STEW

3 tablespoons flour
2 teaspoons chili powder
1½ teaspoons ground cumin
1 pound boneless beef stew, cut into ½-inch pieces
2 tablespoons vegetable oil
2 large onions, cut into ¼-inch wedges
2 cloves garlic, minced
1 14-ounce can beef broth
1 cup beer
⅔ cup picante sauce
1 red bell pepper, cut into ½-inch pieces
   Hot cooked rice (optional)

Combine flour, chili powder, and cumin. Dredge meat in mixture and reserve any remaining flour mixture. Over medium heat, brown meat in oil in Dutch oven. Add onions and garlic; cook and stir 2 minutes. Sprinkle any remaining flour mixture over meat mixture. Cook 1 minute. Add broth, beer, and picante sauce. Bring to a boil. Reduce heat, cover, and simmer approximately 1 hour. Stir in red pepper; continue to simmer, covered, an additional 10 minutes or until beef is tender. Serve with rice and additional picante sauce, if desired. Serves 5-6.

A 31-gallon barrel of beer equals 55 six-packs or 330 12-ounce bottles of beer.

STEWED BEEF

2 tablespoons butter or margarine

1½ pounds beef, cubed

3 tablespoons flour

1 teaspoon minced garlic

1 teaspoon dry mustard

1 12-ounce can beer

1 cup hot water

1 beef bouillon cube

1 bay leaf

⅛ teaspoon marjoram

1 large onion, sliced

1 green pepper, sliced

2 cups sliced mushrooms

Melt butter in large skillet and brown meat; transfer meat to crockpot. Mix together flour, garlic, dry mustard, beer, water, bouillon cube, bay leaf, and marjoram and add to crockpot. Cook on low for 5-6 hours. Add onion, pepper, and mushrooms. Increase heat to medium and cook an additional 2 hours, until meat and vegetables are tender. Serves 4.

When two beer-drinking friends clink their glasses together, they probably are not aware they are making the gesture of banishing the devil by making a "clinking" noise.

TIPSY PORK STEW

1/4 cup flour
1 teaspoon salt
1/4 teaspoon pepper
2 pounds cubed pork,
   shoulder or sirloin
1/4 cup oil
3-4 large onions, sliced
1 clove garlic, minced
1/4 cup chopped fresh parsley
1 teaspoon caraway seeds
1 bay leaf
1 10 1/2-ounce can chicken
   broth
1 12-ounce can beer
1/4 cup red wine vinegar
2 tablespoons brown sugar,
   packed

Combine flour, salt, and pepper in plastic or small brown bag; add meat and shake to coat. Heat oil in Dutch oven and brown meat over medium-high heat. Add onions and garlic. Cook for 5 minutes, stirring occasionally. Pour off drippings. Add remaining ingredients and bring to a boil. Cover and cook over medium heat, approximately 1 3/4 hours, until meat is tender. Stir occasionally. Serves 6-8.

Small beer to a New England colonist did not relate to a quantity but to a quality; small beer had no sugar and was weak—4-5 percent alcohol. It was the most common of all the colonial American beers.

78

MAIN DISHES

79-134

WELSH "BEERBIT"

2 tablespoons butter
2 tablespoons flour
1 cup beer
1½ pounds sharp cheddar cheese, grated
2 eggs
½ teaspoon dry mustard
1 tablespoon Worcestershire sauce
¼ teaspoon white pepper
French bread

Melt butter in a large skillet over low heat; add flour to make roux. Slowly stir in beer. When mixture is smooth and thick, add grated cheese and continue to cook over low heat until cheese is melted. Beat eggs and slowly add to cheese, stirring until eggs thicken—do not overcook! Add Worcestershire and pepper and remove from heat. Pour "Beerbit" over French bread and serve at once. Serves 4.

Many beers have been advertised by beer mats or coasters which have become collectibles; the world's largest collection is reputed to contain approximately 72,000 coasters.

80

ASPARAGUS RAREBIT TOAST

2 tablespoons butter

2 tablespoons flour

2/3 cup flat beer,
    room temperature

1 tablespoon prepared
    mustard

Salt and white pepper to
    taste

2 cups grated sharp cheddar
    cheese

4 slices bread, toasted

12 stalks fresh asparagus,
    cooked and drained

8 strips bacon, fried and
    drained

Pimento, to garnish

In a saucepan over medium-low heat, melt butter. Whisk in flour, stirring constantly for 2-3 minutes until thoroughly blended.

Stir in beer and continue stirring until smooth. Lower heat to lowest setting and stir in mustard, salt, pepper, and cheese; continue on low heat until mixture is smooth and cheese is melted.

Cut toast slices diagonally and arrange on plates, placing 3 stalks of asparagus on each plate. Criss-cross asparagus with bacon; spoon rarebit on top and garnish with pimento. Serves 4.

The first American tavern serving beer to the sailors is said to have been the "Blue Anchor" which was founded in the early 1600's in Philadelphia.

81

BEER CHEESE RAREBIT

2 tablespoons butter
1 pound sharp cheddar
   cheese, shredded
3/4 teaspoon dry mustard
1 tablespoon Worcestershire
   sauce
2 egg yolks
1 cup beer
8 slices toast
   Parsley, garnish

Bring two inches of water in bottom of double boiler to boil over medium heat. Melt butter in top of double boiler. Add cheese to butter and continue cooking, stirring occasionally until cheese is melted. Add seasonings. Beat egg yolks with beer and add to cheese mixture. Cook until thick, stirring occasionally, 5-7 minutes. Serve on toast and garnish with parsley. Serves 6.

The Babylonians made sixteen kinds of beer, using everything from white and black barley to wheat and honey.

CALIFORNIA CRAB RAREBIT

1½   pounds sharp cheddar
     cheese
  2   eggs
  2   tablespoons butter
  2   tablespoons flour
  1   cup flat beer,
     room temperature
  1   tablespoon Worcestershire
     sauce
  ¼   teaspoon pepper
  ¾   teaspoon dry mustard
  1   pound mock crab meat
     French bread
     Chopped parsley and
     paprika, garnish

Grate cheese and set aside. Beat eggs and set aside. Melt butter over low heat in large skillet and gradually add flour to make roux. Slowly stir in beer until mixture is thickened and smooth. Add cheese and continue to cook over low heat. Add eggs, constantly stirring until thick, 5-7 minutes. Add Worcestershire sauce, pepper, and dry mustard. Remove from heat.

To serve, spread crab meat on toasted French bread slices and pour rarebit over all. Garnish with parsley and paprika, if desired. Serves 4.

In the mid 1800's, porter was the most popular beer style in England and also the type brewed by our first president, George Washington. It was first called "intire" but was given the nickname porter because so many of the London porters favored it.

SEAFOOD LASAGNA

8 ounces lasagna noodles
1 tablespoon margarine
2 medium onions, chopped
2 10 3/4-ounce cans cream
  of shrimp soup
1 pound frozen crab meat,
  thawed and drained
1 cup flat beer,
  room temperature
1 cup ricotta cheese
1 8-ounce package cream
  cheese, softened
1 egg, beaten
2 teaspoons basil
1 1 3/4-ounce package dry
  Italian dressing powder
6 ounces raw popcorn shrimp
  (use canned, if desired)
3/4 cup grated Romano cheese
1 pound shrimp,
  cooked and cleaned

Prepare noodles according to package directions. Melt margarine in skillet and saute onion until tender; set aside. In large saucepan, combine soup, crab meat, and beer and bring to boil. Blend ricotta cheese, cream cheese, egg, basil, Italian dressing, and sauteed onion together. Add to hot beer mixture; add popcorn shrimp.

Lightly grease 9 x 13-inch glass cake pan and line bottom with noodles; top with half of sauce and repeat layers. Sprinkle top of dish with Romano cheese. Bake in 350-degree oven for 45 minutes; arrange cooked shrimp on top of dish and return to oven for an additional 15 minutes. Serves 8-10.

Lambic is a rich beer flavored with fruit brewed traditionally in Belgium. The fruit is the basis of the fermentation process.

BEER BATTER FISH

1	12-ounce can beer
1¼	cups flour
¼	cup cornstarch
1	egg
2	teaspoons baking powder
¼	teaspoon paprika
¼	teaspoon garlic powder
3-4	pounds fish fillets
1½	teaspoons salt
	Cooking oil for frying

Combine beer, flour, cornstarch, egg, baking powder, paprika, and garlic powder in bowl and whisk lightly until smooth.

Pat fillets dry with paper towel; lightly sprinkle with salt and coat with batter.

Heat 2-3 inches cooking oil in large skillet to 375-400 degrees. Fry fish on one side for 3-4 minutes; then turn to fry other side an additional 3-4 minutes or until brown. Drain on paper towel. Serves 6-8.

The London Chanticleer *in 1659 paid tribute to the goddesses of cereal and water, the two main ingredients of beer, in this short poem:*

> *Beer is both Ceres,*
> *And good Neptune too!*
> *Beer's froth was the sea*
> *From which Venus grew.*

DEEP FRIED BEER CHICKEN

1½ cups flour
1 tablespoon margarine, melted
1 egg, beaten
1 cup flat beer, room temperature
2 pounds chicken, cut, washed and patted dry
Oil for deep frying

At least four hours before cooking (can be done night before), mix flour, margarine, egg, and sufficient beer to make a thick paste. Spread paste over chicken parts; cover and refrigerate.

Heat 2-3 inches oil in deep fryer to 365 degrees. Fry chicken pieces, a few at a time, for 15-20 minutes or until golden brown. Be sure to move the pieces around in the oil so they do not stick, but turn them carefully so the coating does not break off. Drain on brown bags or paper toweling. Serves 4-5.

In the early 1500's, the technical qualities of fermentation had not been refined, and some batches of beer would turn out badly. In Switzerland the bad batches were blamed on witches, who would be burned at the stake.

FRIED CHICKEN WITH PARSLEY SAUCE

2 tablespoons minced parsley
2/3 cup red wine vinegar
1 teaspoon vegetable oil
   Salt and pepper to taste
1 cup flour
1 cup beer
1½ pounds boneless, skinless
   chicken breast
   Oil for frying

Combine parsley, vinegar, oil, salt, and pepper; set aside. In a separate bowl, whisk together flour, beer, salt, and pepper and blend until smooth. Set aside.

Cut chicken across the grain into ½-inch slices. Heat about 1 inch of oil in a large skillet to 375 degrees. Dip half the chicken pieces in the batter and fry until golden brown, about 4 minutes. Remove with slotted spoon, drain on paper towel, and repeat with remaining chicken. Serve with prepared parsley dipping sauce. Serves 4-6.

Many a beautiful hair style has been treated to beer; flat beer used before, during, or after shampooing will make hair more manageable.

WESTERN TIPSY CHICKEN

1 tablespoon salad oil
1 tablespoon sesame oil
1 broiler/fryer chicken, cut,
  washed and patted dry
1 12-ounce can beer
1/3 cup soy sauce
2/3 cup chopped green onion
1 1/2 tablespoons chopped
  fresh ginger
1 teaspoon oyster sauce
  (optional)
1 clove garlic, minced
2 tablespoons cornstarch
2 tablespoons water
2 tablespoons sesame seeds,
  toasted

In large skillet, place salad oil and sesame oil; heat over medium high heat. Add chicken and cook about 10 minutes, turning to brown on all sides. Remove chicken and arrange in 3-quart baking pan. Drain skillet and discard oil. In skillet, combine beer, soy sauce, onion, ginger, oyster sauce, and garlic; bring to a boil, stirring to loosen brown bits in pan. Pour over chicken and cover. Bake in 350-degree oven for 1 1/2 hours.

Remove chicken to warm serving platter. In small bowl, combine cornstarch and water to make smooth paste. Place baking pan with juices on stove top over medium heat; slowly add cornstarch mixture, stirring constantly to make a thick sauce. Pour over chicken, sprinkle with toasted sesame seeds, and serve. Serves 4-5.

CHICKEN IN TOMATO SAUCE

2 tablespoons margarine
1/2 cup chopped onion
1 10 3/4-ounce can tomato soup
1 12-ounce can beer
1 teaspoon curry powder
1/2 teaspoon oregano
1 2-pound chicken, cut, washed and patted dry
1/4 cup grated Romano cheese

Melt margarine in saucepan and saute onions until tender. Stir in tomato soup, beer, curry powder, and oregano. Simmer, uncovered, for approximately 10 minutes. Arrange chicken in baking dish and pour tomato mixture on top. Bake, uncovered, in 350-degree oven for 1 hour. Sprinkle with Romano cheese before serving. Serves 4-5.

Over 80 million adult Americans enjoy drinking beer each year. Over $4.5 billion dollars were paid by consumers in 1990 for state and federal excise taxes on beer.

In Babylonia the goddess of beer was Siris, and in Egypt the goddess was Isis.

CHICKEN LASAGNA

½ cup margarine
½ cup flour
½ teaspoon basil
½ teaspoon oregano
1½ cups chicken broth
1 12-ounce can beer
3 cups cooked chicken, cubed
2 cups ricotta cheese
1 egg, lightly beaten
6 ounces lasagna noodles, cooked
1 10-ounce package frozen chopped spinach, thawed and drained
8 ounces mozzarella cheese, thinly sliced
¼ cup Romano or parmesan cheese

Make sauce by melting butter in saucepan and mixing with flour, basil, and oregano. Stir in chicken broth and beer. Bring to boiling point, stirring constantly; mixture will become thick. Remove from heat and add chicken and spinach; set aside.

In separate bowl, combine ricotta cheese with egg and mix well. In a greased 9 x 13-inch baking dish, layer one-third of chicken mixture, top with half of ricotta cheese mixture, half of noodles, then half of mozzarella cheese. Repeat layers ending with the last one-third of chicken mixture on top. Top with Romano cheese and bake at 375 degrees for 45 minutes. Serves 6-8.

Many people will acknowledge "a kiss of the hops" is necessary for a good brew, but, perhaps, few know that the states of Idaho, Washington, Oregon, and California produce most of the commercially grown hops.

CHICKEN PILAF

1/4 cup margarine
1/2 cup diced onion
1/2 cup diced green pepper
1 cup uncooked rice or
  brown rice
2 cups beer
1/2 teaspoon salt
1 1/2 cups diced cooked chicken

Melt margarine in a heavy saucepan over moderately low heat. Saute onion and green pepper until tender; add rice and stir-fry about 5 minutes until straw colored. Add beer and salt; cover and cook over lowest heat 18-20 minutes, without stirring, until all liquid is absorbed. Uncover and cook 3-5 minutes longer to dry out. Fluff up with fork; just before serving, add cooked chicken and toss lightly to mix. If chicken is cool, heat before mixing. Serves 6-8.

According to a prominent anthropologist, Dr. Solomon Katz, what lured our ancient ancestors out of their caves may not have been a thirst for knowledge but a thirst for beer. Katz theorizes that when man learned to ferment grain into beer, more than 10,000 years ago, it became one of his most important sources of nutrition. Beer supplied protein that unfermented grain did not, and it tasted better.

STUFFED PORK TENDERLOIN

1 pork tenderloin, approximately 1-1¼ pounds
⅓ cup raisins
1 cup beer
2 tablespoons cider vinegar
½ cup soft pumpernickel bread crumbs
½ cup grated orange rind
2 cloves garlic, minced
2 tablespoons brown sugar
¼ teaspoon pepper
⅛ teaspoon ground cinnamon
2 tablespoons flour
2 tablespoons cold water

Prepare tenderloin by removing all fat and cutting a long slit down center, about ⅔ the way through the meat. Place meat between sheets of heavy-duty plastic wrap or wax paper and flatten to approximately ¼ -inch thick using a rolling pin or meat mallet.

In large shallow non-metal container, combine raisins, beer, and vinegar and add tenderloin, turning to coat. Cover and marinate in refrigerator at least 4 hours, turning occasionally.

In small bowl, combine bread crumbs, orange rind, and garlic; cover and let stand 4 hours.

Remove meat from marinade and place on flat surface. Strain marinade, keeping raisins and discarding liquid. Add raisins to bread crumb mixture. Mix together brown sugar, pepper, and cinnamon and rub evenly over both sides of tenderloin. Spread bread crumb mixture on tenderloin to within 1 inch of edges, patting down firmly. Starting at narrow end, roll up tenderloin like a jelly roll. Tie securely with heavy string approximately 2 inches apart. Place on rack sprayed with vegetable oil in roaster or baking dish. Bake at 400 degrees for approximately 1 hour, until meat is tender.

Transfer meat to platter; remove strings. Mix flour and water to make a paste. Stir paste into pan liquid and heat, stirring until thickened. Slice meat and serve with gravy. Serves 4.

PORK AND SAUERKRAUT

2 tablespoons vegetable oil
3/4 cup chopped onion
1 pound lean pork, cubed
1 12-ounce can beer
1 cup water
1 bay leaf
1/2 teaspoon caraway seed
1/4 teaspoon pepper
1 pound sauerkraut, drained

In 10-inch non-stick skillet, heat oil over medium-high heat; add onion and cook, stirring often until onions are tender. Add pork and brown on all sides. Add beer, water, bay leaf, caraway seed, and pepper and bring to a boil. Reduce heat, cover, and simmer 30 minutes or until pork is tender. Add sauerkraut and cook an additional 20 minutes. Remove bay leaf. Serves 4.

William Penn wrote that the beer in his colony was made of "Molasses...well boyled, with sassafras or Pine infused into it." The taste of such a concoction must have been interesting when drunk out of the popular drinking vessel of the day, a "black jack," which was a waxed, leather tankard.

93

BARBECUED PORK RIBS ON THE GRILL

3 pounds pork spareribs
1 tablespoon chili powder
1/2 teaspoon salt
4 tablespoons vegetable oil, divided
2 cloves garlic, minced
1 1/2 cups finely chopped onions
3/4 cup chili sauce
3/4 cup beer
2 tablespoons cider vinegar
2 teaspoons Tabasco sauce
2 tablespoons brown sugar
Salt and pepper to taste

Cut ribs between bones into single riblet sections and trim away excess fat. Rub chili powder and salt into ribs and let stand at room temperature for at least 1-2 hours. Heat 2 tablespoons oil in 3-4 quart Dutch oven or large casserole over medium-high heat. Brown as many ribs as pan can hold in a single layer; brown well on all sides and remove to drain on paper towels. Repeat with remaining ribs, adding remaining oil as necessary.

When all ribs have been browned, retain about 1 tablespoon oil in pan and add garlic and onion. Saute until lightly browned, stirring occasionally, about 5 minutes. Stir in remaining ingredients and bring to simmering point; add ribs and continue to simmer for approximately 25 minutes. Let cool to room temperature and then put into refrigerator. Marinate for at least 4 hours (or overnight, if desired).

Grill ribs over hot charcoal fire for about 10 minutes, until browned and crusty. Serves 4.

BARBECUED PORK CHOPS

4	pounds pork chops
1	tablespoon oil
2-3	tablespoons liquid smoke
1	cup ketchup
2	tablespoons Worcestershire sauce
1/4	cup vinegar
1/2	cup sugar
1	teaspoon chili powder
1	cup beer
1/4	teaspoon pepper

Brown chops well on each side, a total of about 8-10 minutes, over moderately high heat in skillet brushed with oil. Place browned chops in roasting pan. Place remaining ingredients in small saucepan and bring to boil. Pour over meat; cover with foil wrap and bake at 350 degrees for 1 hour. Uncover, baste with juices in pan, and return to oven for an additional 30 minutes. Serves 6-8.

Long before the days of computerized cash registers, records of drinks purchased were recorded on a board indicating "P" for pints and "Q" for quarts. The tavern owner would remind the barmaids to mind their "P's" and "Q's" so he would get the proper payment.

GERMAN BAKED PORK CHOPS

1 pound sauerkraut, drained
1/2 cup brown sugar
6 smoked pork chops, trimmed of fat
2 medium onions, sliced
2 medium tart apples, pared, cored, and quartered
5 stalks celery, sliced
1 12-ounce can flat beer, room temperature
1 cup ginger ale
1/4 teaspoon fennel
1/4 teaspoon ground cloves
1/4 teaspoon cinnamon
Salt and pepper to taste
1/2 cup dry sherry

Place drained sauerkraut in bottom of 9 x 13-inch cake pan; sprinkle with brown sugar. Layer pork chops on top in a single layer. Cover with onions, apples, and celery; pour beer and ginger ale on top. Sprinkle with spices. Cover pan with foil and bake at 350 degrees for approximately 1 1/2 hours; uncover and pour sherry on top. Return to oven to bake an additional 30 minutes. Serves 6.

The "Beer Barrel Polka" was originally a Czech folk song "Skoda Lasky," which means "lost love."

BAKED PORK CHOPS

1   cup ketchup
1   cup beer
2   tablespoons brown sugar
6   lean loin pork chops,
      about 1/2-inch thick
6   lemon slices

Combine ketchup, beer, and brown sugar in a small bowl and mix well. Place pork chops in a single layer in a baking dish. Place a lemon slice on each piece of meat. Pour sauce over all and bake for 1 hour at 350 degrees. Serves 6.

Joseph Priestly, an English clergyman and chemist who published his discovery of oxygen in 1775, actually came to his conclusions while observing a fermenting vat of beer.

Cerveza is the Spanish word for beer and is derived from the Latin "cerevisia," meaning gift of Ceres, the goddess of agriculture. The English word "beer" comes from the Latin word "bibere," meaning to drink.

PORK CHOPS AND RED CABBAGE

2   tablespoons oil
6   center-cut loin pork chops,
      1/2-inch thick
1/4 teaspoon dried sage
1/4 teaspoon thyme
1/8 teaspoon pepper
1   12-ounce can beer, divided
2   slices bacon, cut in 1-inch
      pieces
4   cups coarsely shredded red
      cabbage
1   cup sliced onions
1/4 cup vinegar
1/4 cup brown sugar, packed
2   cups sliced pears

Place oil in large skillet and brown pork chops over medium-high heat. Season with sage, thyme, and pepper. Add 1 cup of beer; cover and cook over medium-low heat for approximately 1 hour, until meat is tender.

While meat is cooking, fry bacon in Dutch oven until crisp; add cabbage and onions. Cook and stir over medium heat for 5 minutes. Add remaining beer, vinegar, and brown sugar and mix well. Cover and simmer over low heat for 15 minutes. Add pears and bring to a boil. Serve pork chops nestled on bed of cabbage mixture. Serves 6.

Experienced beer drinkers can taste the difference between beer stored in wooden barrels and beer stored in aluminum kegs; the drinking container—can, stein, or glass—can also make a difference to a true beer connoisseur.

PORK CHOPS AND MUSHROOMS

6 pork chops, rib or sirloin
2 tablespoons oil
1 10³/₄-ounce can cream of
mushroom soup
1 1-ounce envelope onion
soup mix
1 cup beer
1 8-ounce can mushrooms

Remove fat from pork chops. Heat oil in large skillet and brown pork chops for about 10 minutes, turning at least once to brown both sides. Remove chops and set aside. In skillet, combine soup, soup mix, and beer and cook over low heat, stirring to loosen browned bits. Return pork chops to pan, spooning some sauce over chops. Bring to a boil; reduce heat and simmer covered 1-1¹/₂ hours, until meat is tender. Add mushrooms and simmer for an additional 5 minutes. Serve with buttered noodles and garnish with parsley. Serves 6.

If 162 12-ounce bottles equal a half barrel of beer, would there be more or fewer servings of 12-ounce glasses in a half barrel? The correct answer is more glasses of beer because the foam, called "head" or "collar" that forms on a glass of beer, takes space.

PORK CHOPS WITH ONION-BEER SAUCE

1/2 teaspoon pepper
3 tablespoons flour
6 pork chops, rib or sirloin
2 tablespoons vegetable oil
3 medium onions, sliced
1 cup beer
1/2 cup hot beef broth or
   bouillon
1 1/2 teaspoons cornstarch
2-3 tablespoons cold water

Add pepper to flour and dredge pork chops on both sides. Heat oil in heavy skillet and brown pork chops on both sides. Add onions and cook an additional 5 minutes, turning meat once. Add beer and broth, cover, and simmer for approximately 12 minutes, until pork chops are tender. Remove meat to platter and keep warm.

Mix cornstarch in cold water to form thin paste and stir into sauce; cook until thick. Serve sauce over pork chops. Serves 6.

The American brewing industry was well established in 1770; George Washington, Patrick Henry and other patriots argued for a boycott of English beer imports. The Boston Tea Party could have become the "Boston Beer Party."

100

BAVARIAN PORK CHOPS

4 boneless loin pork chops,
   approximately 1/2-inch
   thick
3/4 cup flour
1 tablespoon butter or
   margarine
1/2 pound fresh mushrooms,
   sliced
1/2 teaspoon thyme
1/2 cup chopped green onions
2 cloves garlic, minced
1 cup beer, room temperature
   Salt and pepper to taste

Dredge pork chops lightly in flour. Melt butter or margarine in heavy skillet over medium-high heat. Brown meat on both sides quickly; remove from pan and set aside. In same pan, saute mushrooms and thyme about 1 minute. Return chops to pan; add onions and garlic. Add beer and bring to a boil. Reduce heat, cover, and simmer until meat is tender, approximately 1 hour. Season to taste. Delicious served over buttered noodles and garnished with parsley. Serves 4.

At Heriot-Watt University in Edinburgh, Scotland, some students take their beer very seriously; one can major in brewing and get a bachelor's degree in the craft.

Draught beer is beer in a cask or barrel rather than beer in a bottle.

BEEF BURGERS

2 pounds ground chuck
3 tablespoons onion soup mix
   (powder and flakes)
1 cup beer
   Salt and pepper to taste

Mix ground chuck, soup mix, and beer. Form into thick patties and season with salt and pepper. Grill on foil over glowing coals or broil on rack in oven. Serves 6-8.

Note: To prepare grilled cheeseburgers use 3/4 cup beer and add 1/2 cup grated cheddar cheese.

A 12-ounce bottle of beer contains 150 calories. The same amount of whole milk is 240 calories, 2 pieces of bread are 170 calories, and a cup of cottage cheese is 160 calories. Beer may be the diet drink of the future!!

BEER-B-CUED BEEF

5   pounds ground beef
2   large onions, diced
1   heaping tablespoon paprika
1   tablespoon dried mustard
1/4 teaspoon crushed red pepper
1   heaping tablespoon chili
     powder
1   tablespoon pepper
1/4 cup Worcestershire sauce
1   tablespoon vinegar
1   12-ounce can beer
2   cups ketchup
1   cup tomato juice
1   cup flour (approximately)

Brown beef over low heat in a large pan; add all other ingredients except flour. Mix well and add flour to thicken to desired consistency. Simmer over low heat 30 minutes, stirring occasionally. Serve on potato or hamburger buns. Serves 25-30.

In early Europe people referred to beer as "liquid bread" because the basic ingredients and processes are very similar.

SLOPPY JOES

4 tablespoons vegetable oil, divided
4 medium red onions, chopped
2 large red peppers, chopped
6 cloves garlic, minced
1 teaspoon salt
1/2 teaspoon pepper
1/2 teaspoon thyme
3 pounds lean ground beef
2 cups chili sauce
2 cups beer
1/3 cup Worcestershire sauce
1/2 teaspoon Tabasco sauce
10 large sesame rolls
1/4 cup plus 2 tablespoons finely sliced scallion greens

Heat 2 tablespoons oil in large skillet over medium heat. Add onions, peppers, garlic, salt, pepper, and thyme and cook, stirring occasionally until onion is tender but not brown, about 10 minutes. Remove onion mixture with slotted spoon to plate. Add remaining oil and increase heat slightly. Add meat and cook for about 3-4 minutes, breaking pieces into small particles. Add onion mixture, chili sauce, beer, Worcestershire sauce, and Tabasco sauce and stir well. Heat to simmering; reduce heat and simmer partially covered until flavors blend and sauce thickens slightly, about 15-18 minutes.

Toast rolls in broiler with cut side up; place on serving plates, sprinkle with scallions, and spoon meat mixture over rolls. Serve hot. Serves 20.

ITALIAN BEEF

4-5 pounds boneless chuck
    roast
 4 tablespoons margarine or
    butter
   Garlic powder to taste
   Salt and pepper to taste
   Oregano to taste
 4 tablespoons onion flakes
 2 11½-ounce jars
    peperoncini peppers,
    drained, reserve juice
 1 10½-ounce can beef broth
 1 12-ounce can beer

Cut chuck roast into 2-inch cubes and brown in melted margarine in skillet. Remove browned pieces of meat and place in crockpot or slow cooker. Add garlic powder, salt, pepper, oregano, onion flakes, and peppers. Pour in broth, pepper juice, and beer. Cover and cook on low overnight, 8-10 hours, until meat is tender and can be shredded with fork. Remove stems from peppers, shred beef, and return all to crockpot. Serve with juices on hard rolls. Serves 15-17.

Two beer drinkers of note are Auguste Maffrey of France who drank 12 quarts of beer in 52 minutes in 1952, and J.H. Cochrane who drank 2 liters of beer in 11 seconds in 1932.

BAR-B-CUE BEEF

3   pounds boneless chuck
    roast
3   tablespoons oil
1   cup diced onion
1/2 cup diced celery
3   tablespoons vinegar
3   tablespoons brown sugar
11/4 cups ketchup
4   tablespoons A-1 steak
    sauce
4   tablespoons chili powder
1   12-ounce can beer
1/4 cup lemon juice

Cut meat into 2-inch squares and brown in oil in skillet. Transfer to baking pan and top with onion and celery. In separate bowl, blend all remaining ingredients and pour over top of meat. Cover and bake at 350 degrees for 3 hours or until meat is tender enough to shred with fork. Shred and return meat to pan; blend with juices and cook an additional 45 minutes. Serve on potato buns.

If there is any mixture left over, you can mix it with sour cream for an easy stroganoff. Serves 18-22.

Many beer tankards have a glass bottom; this dates back to early Colonial times when anyone who drank a beer into which a coin had been dropped unwittingly accepted a shilling from the King and automatically became a member of the Imperial Forces. A glass-bottomed tankard was the answer.

HOT BEEF SANDWICHES

4-5 pounds boneless chuck
   roast
½ cup margarine or butter
3 10¾-ounce cans cream of
   mushroom soup
½ cup dried onion flakes
1 cup beer

Cut chuck roast in 2-inch cubes and brown several pieces at a time in melted margarine or butter in skillet. As pieces are browned, remove to crockpot and repeat until all meat is done. Add soup, onion flakes, and beer to crockpot and cook overnight, 6-8 hours. Remove meat from crockpot and flake with fork; return to crockpot and mix thoroughly with juices. Can be kept hot until ready to serve. Serve with soft buns. Serves 24-28.

In early England the "jet set" life of today would probably have been described as "life of beer and skittles," meaning drink and play—a life of easy enjoyment.

107

FRANKFURTERS AND BEER

2 frankfurters
2 frankfurter buns
  Mustard, ketchup, and
    pickles
1 six-pack beer

Grill frankfurters on backyard grill, put between buns, and smother with mustard, ketchup, and pickles. Eat up and drink the beer down!

Malt is the by-product of barley grain, which is a natural source of carbohydrates, enzymes, and flavor compounds.

In Charles Dickens' "Old Curiosity Shop," the small servant is asked, "Did you ever taste beer?" Her answer is, "I had a sip of it once." The character Mr. Swiveller rebuts with the statement: "She never tasted it—it cannot be tasted in a sip."

BRATWURST AND ONIONS

1½   12-ounce cans beer
2   pounds bratwurst
2   large onions, sliced
4   peppercorns
4   tablespoons margarine
1   tablespoon Worcestershire
    sauce

Pour beer into large saucepan and add bratwurst, onions, and peppercorns. Bring to boil, reduce heat, and simmer for 20 minutes. Drain, reserving bratwurst and onions.

Grill bratwurst on grill until browned. Brown onions in melted margarine in skillet with Worcestershire sauce. Serve bratwurst and onions on brat rolls or similar hard roll. Serves 6-8.

George Washington had his own brewhouse, and his recipe for beer, in his own handwriting, is in the archives of the New York Public Library.

BRATS AND KRAUT

6   bratwurst patties, grilled
1   16-ounce can sauerkraut
1   large onion, diced
1   cup beer

Place grilled bratwurst patties in aluminum foil pan and cover with sauerkraut and onions. Pour beer on top. Simmer over charcoal grill or in oven for 30 minutes. Serve patties, sauerkraut, and onions on buns. Serves 6.

A "growler" is a quart bucket that was used to carry beer from an opened barrel to the customer. This beer foamed more than beer from a freshly opened barrel and the customer usually was not happy. "Growler" was the nickname given to the customer who felt he did not get his full amount and complained.

MEATBALLS IN BEER

2 cups lightly packed bread crumbs
1 1/3 cups beer, divided
2 tablespoons butter or margarine
1/2 pound ground chuck
1/2 pound ground pork
1 small onion, minced
1 egg
1/8 teaspoon cayenne pepper
1/4 teaspoon nutmeg
1 teaspoon lemon juice

Soak bread cubes in 1/3 cup beer. Melt butter or margarine in skillet and saute onions. In a separate bowl, combine meat, onions, bread crumbs that have been squeezed, egg, cayenne pepper, and nutmeg. Form into 2-inch balls and brown in drippings left in skillet after removing onions (if necessary, add more butter or margarine); brown all sides. Add remaining 1 cup beer and lemon juice and cover; simmer for 30 minutes.

Remove meat from pan and reduce juices to serve with meat. Serves 4.

134,400,000 twelve-ounce bottles or cans of beer would float the U.S.S. Missouri, which weighs 45,000 long tons.

111

BEER STUFFED PEPPERS

4 large green peppers
3 tablespoons butter
1/4 cup diced celery
2 green onions, chopped
1/2 pound ground beef
1/2 cup whole kernel corn,
    drained
1/2 cup finely chopped tomatoes
4 cups stale bread, cubed
1/2 teaspoon salt
    Dash of pepper
1/2 cup beer, divided

Trim tops of peppers; remove core and seeds and blanch them by boiling in hot water for about 5 minutes. Remove from heat and drain; set aside.

Heat butter in saucepan and saute celery, onions, and meat until meat is browned. Add corn, chopped tomatoes, bread cubes, salt, and pepper and toss lightly to mix. Blend in 1/4 cup beer. Spoon stuffing into green peppers. Place in a deep baking dish and pour rest of beer into the bottom around peppers. Cover with foil and bake in a 350-degree oven for 1 hour. Serves 4.

"Have a beer"—a welcome invitation in any language you say it; the word for beer in Spanish is "cerveza," in Japanese it is "biru," and in French you would say "biere." The Germans call it "bier."

112

MEAT AND POTATO CASSEROLE

2 pounds ground beef chuck
2 tablespoons margarine, divided
4 medium onions, sliced
1/2 cup water
8-9 medium potatoes, peeled and sliced 1/4-inch thick
Salt and pepper to taste
1/2 cup beer
Minced parsley, for garnish

Form ground chuck into 10 patties; set aside. Melt 1 tablespoon margarine in skillet and saute onions until lightly browned; remove from pan and set aside. Add remaining margarine to skillet and brown meat patties. Remove meat. Add water to pan and loosen drippings for 2-3 minutes; set aside.

Grease 2-quart casserole dish and spread half of potatoes on bottom; season with salt and pepper. Cover with meat patties topped with onions and season as desired. Cover with remaining potatoes; pour on pan drippings and beer. Cover with foil and bake at 375 degrees for 1 1/2 hours. Garnish with parsley. Serves 6-8.

In Europe in the Middle Ages, beer was considered safer to drink than water (which was often questionable) because the brewing process killed any bacteria that may have been present.

113

"SHORTY'S MEATLOAF"

2 pounds lean ground beef
2 8-ounce envelopes
   spaghetti sauce mix
1 cup beer
1 tablespoon minced onion
1/4 teaspoon minced garlic
1 cup bread stuffing

Combine all ingredients. Mix well and shape into loaf. Place in pan and bake in 350-degree oven for 1 hour.

Note: Ingredients can be shaped into meatballs, placed in a single layer on pan, and baked at 350 degrees for 20 minutes. Serves 6.

"Helles" and "Dunkels" sound like they refer to the home of the devil and something to dip into coffee. On the contrary, they are German terms for light and dark beers.

Beer heated with a red-hot poker that is popular in winter is called "poker beer" and is best to drink sitting around a fire after skiing.

GERMAN MEAT PIE

1/2 teaspoon pepper
1 teaspoon sage
1/2 teaspoon salt
1/3 cup flour
3 pounds boneless beef chuck,
   trimmed and cut into
   1-2-inch cubes
4 tablespoons vegetable oil
2 tablespoons butter or
   margarine, divided
3 cups chopped onions
2 large cloves garlic, minced
1/2 teaspoon thyme
1 bay leaf
3 medium potatoes, peeled
   and cubed
4 medium carrots, cut into
   1-inch pieces
1/4 pound mushrooms, sliced
1/4 cup tomato paste
1/4 cup minced parsley
1 12-ounce can beer
1 cup strong coffee
1 cup plus 1 tablespoon water
   Pastry for single crust pie
1 egg

In brown bag, mix pepper, sage, salt, and flour. Place beef cubes in bag and shake to cover; shake portions of meat at a time so all sides are dusted. If necessary, add additional flour. In large oven-proof saucepan, heat vegetable oil and 1 tablespoon butter or margarine. Brown meat on all sides; again it will be necessary to do this in portions.

When meat is browned, remove with slotted spoon and set aside. Add remaining butter, onions, and garlic to same saucepan and saute for about 5 minutes. Add thyme and bay leaf. Mix in vegetables, tomato paste, parsley, beer, coffee, and 1 cup water. Bring to a boil. Return meat to pan, cover, and put in preheated 325-degree oven for approximately 1 1/2 hours. If saucepan is not oven-proof, transfer all to baking dish before placing in oven.

Roll and cut pastry to fit top of casserole; set aside. Transfer meat mixture to casserole and cover meat mixture with pastry. Combine egg and remaining 1 tablespoon water; brush egg glaze on pastry. Cut slits in top and finish edges as you would for pie. Return to oven and bake at 325 degrees for 1 hour, until crust is browned and meat mixture is bubbling. Serves 6-8.

BREWED BEEF ON NOODLES

4　tablespoons vegetable oil, divided
3　large onions, sliced
4　pounds boneless beef chuck, cubed into 2-inch pieces
3　tablespoons flour
1　12-ounce can beer
3/4　cup water
2　cubes beef bouillon
1　bay leaf
1　teaspoon sugar
1/2　teaspoon thyme
1/2　teaspoon salt
1/4　teaspoon basil
1/8　teaspoon pepper
　　Hot cooked noodles
　　Parsley, chives, or chopped green onion, garnish

Heat 2 tablespoons vegetable oil in 4-quart oven-proof skillet or Dutch oven, over medium heat. Add onions; cook and stir until golden and tender. Remove onions with slotted spoon; reserve. In skillet, brown meat on all sides. Remove meat; reserve.

Add remaining oil to skillet. Add flour, stirring until browned. Gradually add beer and water; cook and stir until slightly thickened. Stir in bouillon, bay leaf, sugar, thyme, salt, basil, and pepper.

Add reserved beef and onions, stirring to combine. Cover and bake in 350-degree oven for 2 hours or until beef is tender and gravy thickened. Remove bay leaf. Serve over hot noodles and garnish with parsley, chives, or onion. Serves 10.

BEEF 'N' BREW

3 pounds beef chuck, cubed
1/4 cup flour
1/2 cup butter or margarine
1/4 cup chopped parsley
1 teaspoon thyme
1 bay leaf
2 tablespoons wine vinegar
2 12-ounce cans beer
6 medium onions, sliced
1 teaspoon brown sugar
1/2 teaspoon salt
1/2 teaspoon black pepper

Dredge beef in flour or place flour and meat in a plastic bag, shaking bag to coat. Melt butter in heavy skillet with a cover and brown meat cubes; add all remaining ingredients. Bring to boil, then simmer covered for 1 hour until meat is tender. Remove bay leaf. Serve with rice or noodles. Serves 6.

One of the first recorded references to beer appears on an Assyrian tablet, which names it as a supply aboard Noah's ark.

The first beer steins were made in Germany out of stone. Stein is the German word for stone.

117

BEEF AND BEER

1-1½ pounds boneless beef chuck, sliced ¼-inch thick

Salt and pepper to taste

¾ cup butter or margarine, divided

1½ cups thinly sliced onions

3 cups beer

1 herb bouquet (piece of celery, sprig of thyme, 3 or 4 sprigs of parsley, and a bay leaf tied together; or enmeshed cheesecloth)

½ cup flour

2 teaspoons brown sugar

Season meat slices with salt and pepper to taste. In heavy skillet, melt ¼ cup butter or margarine and brown meat on both sides; remove meat from skillet and set aside. Brown onions in skillet and remove with slotted spoon. In large saucepan, alternate layers of meat and onions.

To juice in skillet, add beer and herb bouquet and keep warm. In a separate bowl, make a roux-like paste using flour, ½ cup softened butter, and brown sugar. Add small amount of hot beer mixture to roux and blend until smooth. Add roux slowly to beer mixture, cooking and stirring until thick and smooth.

Pour over layered beef and onions and bring to boil; cover and simmer over low heat for 2-2½ hours, until meat is tender. Serve over hot noodles. Serves 4-5.

118

BREADED BEEF IN BEER

3   pounds beef chuck, cubed
4   tablespoons butter or
      margarine
3   tablespoons flour
1   cup sliced onions
2   cups beer
1/2 teaspoon thyme
1/4 teaspoon nutmeg
1   teaspoon salt
12-15 slices French bread
4   tablespoons Dijon
      mustard

Brown meat in butter; transfer to covered casserole and sprinkle with flour. Add onions, beer, and seasonings. Cover tightly and bake for 2 hours at 350 degrees.

Remove casserole from oven and cover with slices of bread which have been spread with mustard, placing mustard side down on meat. Return uncovered casserole dish to oven and bake an additional 20 minutes. Serves 4.

Archaeologists discovered a 4,000-year-old Mesopotamian clay tablet, and after deciphering its cryptic markings, it turned out to be a recording of a recipe for beer—not just any recipe but a formula handed down from the god Enki.

It is said that when Caesar crossed the Rubicon, he toasted his troops with beer; his pack animals always carried a good supply of beer on his marches.

119

BOILED BEEF AND CABBAGE

3½ pounds trimmed beef
     brisket
4   peppercorns
2   bay leaves
1   clove garlic, minced
1   12-ounce can beer,
     approximately
2   pounds small red potatoes
1   cup peeled and diagonally
     sliced carrots
1   medium cabbage, cored
     and cut into 8 wedges
1   cup thinly sliced onion

In 8-inch Dutch oven over high heat, heat brisket, peppercorns, bay leaves, garlic, and enough beer to cover. Bring to boil. Reduce heat to low, cover, and simmer about 3 hours, until meat is fork-tender. Remove brisket from Dutch oven and keep warm.

Taste brisket cooking liquid; if too salty, discard and replace with approximately same amount of fresh water or beer. Add potatoes and carrots and boil over high heat; reduce heat, cover, and simmer 20 minutes. Add cabbage and onion and cook an additional 10 minutes or until all vegetables are tender.

To serve, arrange brisket and vegetables on platter. Serves 6-8.

A barrel holds 31 gallons of beer or 3,968 ounces of beer; there are 12 ounces in a can of beer, or 330 cans of beer per barrel.

BEEF, BEER 'N' KRAUT

3 tablespoons bacon
  drippings
1 cup sliced onion
3 pounds beef brisket
2 pounds sauerkraut
1½ 12-ounce cans beer,
  room temperature
Salt and pepper to taste
½ teaspoon caraway seeds
  (optional)

In large skillet or saucepan, heat bacon drippings; add onion and lightly brown. Add meat and put sauerkraut on top; pour beer over and bring to boil. Reduce heat and simmer, covered, for 2½-3 hours, until meat is tender. Add salt and pepper and caraway seeds. Serves 6.

When Rear Admiral Byrd took his expedition to the Antarctic in 1933-1935, he stocked beer because he declared it provided minerals and other dietetic supplements lacking in melted snow.

BRISKET IN BREW

1   12-ounce can beer
1   bay leaf
2   cloves garlic
1/2   teaspoon sage
1/4   teaspoon dry mustard
1   teaspoon salt
4-5   pounds beef brisket
2   tablespoons butter or
     margarine
2   tablespoons flour

Mix beer, bay leaf, split garlic cloves, and spices to make marinade. Place meat in shallow baking dish and pour marinade over meat; cover dish. Marinate overnight in refrigerator.

In Dutch oven or heavy covered skillet, melt butter over intense heat. Remove meat from marinade; pat dry with paper toweling. Brown meat on all sides. Discard garlic pieces from marinade and pour over meat. Cover and simmer on medium heat for 2-3 hours, until meat is tender.

Remove meat and strain liquid; skim fat from surface and return liquid to pan. Remove 2-3 tablespoons of liquid and mix with flour to make a roux. Add roux to remaining liquid in pan and cook until thickened. Slice meat across grain and return to pan and reheat. Serves 8.

122

TANGY BEEF IN BEER

4 pounds boneless rump roast
Salt and pepper to taste
2/3 cup sliced onion
1/3 cup chili sauce
3 tablespoons brown sugar
1 teaspoon minced garlic
1 12-ounce can beer,
room temperature

Season meat with salt and pepper to taste and place in baking dish (9 x 13-inch cake pan works fine); place onion slices on meat. Mix remaining ingredients together and pour over roast. Cover with foil and bake for approximately 2½ hours at 350 degrees, until meat is tender; remove cover for last half hour and baste at 10-minute intervals. Serves 8.

Our country's first "help wanted" sign was posted in London in 1609 appealing for brewers to work in Virginia.

History shows that the oldest beer mash was found in the Town of Alzey in Germany. The chemical breakdown of a dark brown substance found there indicated it was a beer mash that had been tightly closed, thereby retaining its basic qualities for 16 centuries.

123

EASY ENTREE—BEEF IN BEER

2 pounds boneless chuck
   roast
1/4 teaspoon garlic powder
1/4 cup flour
   Salt and pepper to taste
1/4 cup oil
1 medium onion, sliced
1 10-ounce can tomato sauce
1 cup beer, room temperature

Cut meat into 2-inch cubes, removing as much fat as possible. Combine garlic powder, flour, salt, and pepper in plastic bag; add meat and shake to coat meat with mixture. Heat oil in skillet and brown meat on all sides. Remove meat and place in crockpot. Saute onions in skillet. Pour onions, tomato sauce, and beer over meat. Cover and cook on low for 7-9 hours, until meat is tender. Juice may be thickened with flour/water paste to form gravy. Delicious served over buttered noodles or rice. Serves 5-6.

A fired-baked clay tablet, written in Sumerian and Akkadian in about the 4th or 5th century B.C., indicates the Babylonians may have had more kinds of beer than we have now—dark beer, pale beer, red beer, three-fold beer, beer with a head, and one without to name a few.

EASY POT ROAST

4   pounds sirloin tip or
     rump roast
1   1-ounce package onion
     soup mix
1   12-ounce can beer,
     approximately
5   medium potatoes,
     peeled and cut
5   small carrots,
     scraped and cut
3   stalks celery, diced
2   tablespoons flour
1/2 cup cold water

Put roast in pan, sprinkle with soup mix, and pour beer over roast. Cover and bake in 350-degree oven for 2 1/2 hours. Add potatoes, carrots, and celery and bake an additional 45-60 minutes, until meat and vegetables are tender. Add additional beer, if necessary, to make sure there is sufficient liquid to avoid vegetables sticking to pan. Mix flour with cold water and add to juices to make gravy. Serves 8-10.

In 1965 the first privately endowed college for women was given endowment money by Matthew Vassar, a brewer in Poughkeepsie, New York. The Academy for Women was later renamed Vassar College in his honor.

125

BEERBRATEN WITH GINGER GRAVY

4 pounds beef rump roast
2 medium onions, thinly sliced
4 peppercorns
4 cloves
1 bay leaf
1 cup white vinegar
2 cups beer, divided
1/2 cup cider vinegar
1/4 cup vegetable oil
1/2 teaspoon salt
1/2 cup boiling water
10 gingersnap cookies
1/2 cup sour half-and-half
1 tablespoon flour

Place beef roast in deep glass container. Add onions, peppercorns, cloves, and bay leaf. Pour white vinegar, 1 cup beer, and cider vinegar over the meat; chill, covered in refrigerator for 72 hours. Turn meat twice each 24 hours.

Remove roast from marinade and wipe dry with paper towel. Strain marinade into bowl, reserving 1 cup marinade and onion slices.

Heat vegetable oil in Dutch oven and brown roast on all sides, seasoning with salt. Pour water and remaining beer over meat and sprinkle in crushed gingersnap cookies. Simmer covered for 1 1/2 hours, turning often. Add reserved marinade and onions; cook an additional 2 hours, until meat is tender. Remove roast and keep warm. Strain juices into saucepan.

Blend sour half-and-half with flour in small bowl and add to juices in saucepan, stirring until gravy is thickened and smooth. Slice meat in thin slices and add to hot gravy. Arrange meat on platter and serve with additional gravy. Serves 10.

BREWED ROAST

4 pounds rump or sirloin tip
   roast

4 tablespoons margarine or
   butter

1 20-ounce bottle tomato
   ketchup

1 12-ounce can beer

1 large onion, thinly sliced

In large skillet or saucepan, brown roast in margarine. Mix ketchup, beer, and onion together and pour over meat. Simmer covered for 2 hours. Uncover and simmer for 1 more hour, until meat is tender. Serves 6-8.

Wort is the liquid that results from the steeping of malt during the brewing process. Yeast is added to cause fermentation, producing natural carbon dioxide and alcohol.

"Beery Christmas"—In 1993 Howard Schmaling III of Kenosha, Wisconsin, created a 4-foot tall Christmas tree entirely out of 50,000 steel beer-bottle caps. In 1994, he used double that number, 100,852 to be exact, to create a 6-foot tall tree.

UNCLE OTTO'S POT ROAST

6 pounds boneless chuck roast
2 tablespoons butter or margarine
2 cups water
1 12-ounce can beer
1 cup canned tomatoes
1 tablespoon cider vinegar
1 large onion, chopped
2 tablespoons brown sugar
1 teaspoon salt
1 teaspoon cinnamon
1/2 teaspoon ginger
1 bay leaf
6 tablespoons flour

Brown meat in melted butter in heavy skillet or Dutch oven. Combine water, beer, tomatoes, vinegar, onion, sugar, and spices and pour over meat. Cover and simmer for about 3-4 hours, until meat is tender. Carve meat and place on warm platter.

Strain liquid and add enough flour to thicken to gravy. Serves 8-10.

The movie "Strange Brew," filmed in 1983, had in its cast an evil brewmaster who was attempting to take over the world by addicting beer drinkers to a drug-laced beer; a character who is saved from drowning in a beer storage tank by his unsatiable thirst; and, a beer drinking dog named Hosehead.

GRILLED FLANK STEAK

1 cup beer, room temperature
1/2 cup oil
1/4 teaspoon garlic powder
1/4 teaspoon pepper
1 tablespoon lemon juice
2 pounds flank steak

Combine all ingredients except steak and mix well. Put steak in flat, glass dish and pour marinade over top; cover. (You can use glass cake pan and cover with plastic wrap.) Refrigerate for 24 hours or keep at room temperature 4-5 hours. Turn steak occasionally.

Broil on grill 3 inches from heat for 8 minutes each side. Slice diagonally and enjoy. Serves 6-8.

The ripple effect of the beer industry on the United States' economy is tremendous. It provides an estimated 187,000 jobs in production and distribution, plus the employment of thousands of other workers in providing the raw materials for processing the beer and manufacturing its packaging.

CROCKED BEEF

1 cup flour
3 pounds round steak, cubed
1 12-ounce can beer
1 1-ounce envelope onion soup mix
1 .87-ounce envelope brown gravy mix
1½ cups sliced mushrooms

Put flour in a bag and add meat; shake bag well to coat meat. Combine beer and mixes in crockpot; stir and add meat. Cover and cook on low for 8 hours; add mushrooms the last hour. Delicious served over rice or noodles. Serves 6.

"Grace Before Beers" Higgins 1580

For what this house affords us,
Come, praise the brewers most—
Who caught into a bottle
The barley's gentle ghost
Until our parching throttles
In silence we employ
Like geese that drink a mouthful
Then stretch their necks with joy!

OVEN STEAK

4 tablespoons butter or
   margarine
2 pounds round steak,
   1-inch thick
1/2 cup flour
1 large onion, chopped
1 cup beer
   Salt and pepper to taste
1 bay leaf
1 teaspoon parsley
1/4 teaspoon thyme

Preheat oven to 275 degrees. Melt butter or margarine in oven-proof skillet over medium heat. Coat steak with flour and brown on both sides. Remove meat and set aside.

Add onion to skillet and saute until glazed. Remove approximately half of onions, add meat, and cover with remaining onions. Add beer, salt and pepper, bay leaf, parsley, and thyme. Cover and bake in oven for about 2 hours, until meat is tender. Remove bay leaf before serving. Serves 4.

*Charlemagne the Great was the personal tutor
and trainer of the brewers in his kingdom.*

131

BEER-BASTED BEEF STEAK

¼ cup brown sugar
2 tablespoons prepared
    German-style mustard
1 tablespoon vinegar
1 teaspoon salt
¼ teaspoon coarsely ground
    pepper
1 cup beer
1 medium onion, chopped
1 bay leaf
1 top round beef steak,
    1-inch thick

Combine brown sugar, mustard, vinegar, salt, and pepper in saucepan over low heat; slowly stir in beer. Add onion and bay leaf and cook slowly 10 minutes, stirring occasionally. Cool.

Place steak in plastic bag; add marinade, turning to coat. Tie bag securely and marinate in refrigerator 6-8 hours (or overnight), turning at least once. Drain marinade from steak; reserve marinade. Broil steak over low to medium heat for 22 minutes for rare; 26 minutes for medium. Turn once. Brush with reserved marinade occasionally. Carve in thin slices. Serves 4.

If you are in a tavern and a customer asks for a "boiler-maker," don't expect to see the man in charge of the heating system. The customer is ordering a drink—a shot of whiskey and a beer.

132

BARBECUED T-BONE STEAK

1 cup ketchup
1 cup beer
3 tablespoons light brown
   sugar
3 tablespoons cider vinegar
3 tablespoons Worcestershire
   sauce
3 teaspoons chili powder
1 clove garlic, minced
   Dash ground red pepper
3 1-pound T-bone steaks

In medium saucepan, combine ketchup, beer, brown sugar, vinegar, Worcestershire sauce, chili powder, garlic, and red pepper. Bring to a boil over medium-high heat. Reduce heat and simmer until thickened, stirring occasionally. Remove from heat and cool to room temperature.

Trim excess fat from steaks. Pierce meat on both sides with fork. Place steaks in large shallow baking dish. Pour sauce over steaks turning to coat well. Cover and refrigerate at least 4 hours or overnight, turning occasionally.

Heat grill or broiler. Remove steaks from sauce and place on grill or broiler rack. Cook 4 inches from heat source for 4 minutes on each side for rare, or 8 minutes on each side for well-done, brushing with any remaining sauce while cooking. Serves 3.

Note: If you prefer not to marinate steaks, brush sauce on steaks while grilling.

BEERY GOOD VENISON

2½-3 pounds venison roast
1 1-ounce package onion
   soup mix
1 12-ounce can beer

Trim all fat from roast and put in slow cooker. Sprinkle onion soup mix on meat and pour in beer. Cook on low heat for 8-10 hours, until meat is tender. Serves 5-7.

*A "tavern tale" is a story told while enjoying
a glass of beer; the story is usually fiction.*

Lager beer gets its name from the German word "lagern" meaning to store. During the 7th century, monks discovered that their beer kept better in the summer if stored in cool mountain caves. Monks found that beer mellowed after standing for a time. Aging beer grew out of this practice.

SAUCES

135-146

MARINADE BREW

1   12-ounce can beer
1/2   cup vegetable oil
2   tablespoons cider vinegar
1/2   cup chopped onion
2   cloves garlic, minced
1/2   teaspoon salt

Blend all ingredients together. Cover meat to be marinated and let stand in refrigerator overnight. Turn meat at least once or twice. Makes sufficient to cover 2 pounds meat, approximately 2 cups.

An often-used toast: "Here's to a long life and a merry one, A happy one and a cheery one, A pretty girl and an honest one, A cold beer and then another one."

136

BEER MARINADE FOR TURKEY

3 cups pineapple juice
1 12-ounce can beer, chilled
3 tablespoons molasses
1/8 teaspoon onion powder
1/8 teaspoon garlic powder
1/8 teaspoon cinnamon
3 tablespoons brown sugar
6 tablespoons butter or
   margarine, melted
Salt and pepper to taste

Mix all the ingredients together. Put turkey in large plastic bag (a garbage or waste paper bag will do) and pour marinade over. Tie bag and place in refrigerator on cookie sheet for minimum of 12 hours, turning turkey periodically. Roast as desired. Covers one 12-15-pound turkey, approximately 5 cups.

November 2, the Feast of St. Martin, is a day that should be celebrated by all tavern keepers. St. Martin is the patron saint of tavern keepers.

BEER MARINADE FOR WILD GAME

1   12-ounce can beer
1/4   cup plus 2 tablespoons
     cider vinegar
1   bay leaf
2   tablespoons Worcestershire
     sauce
2   whole cloves
     Pinch of salt

Mix all ingredients together. Pour in plastic bag and marinate any type of wild game for 6-8 hours, turning once. Covers 3-5 pounds meat, approximately 2 cups.

When George Washington, the epitome of honest politicians, ran for election to the House of Burgesses, he wooed the voters with festivities that included "30 gallons of strong beer."

MILWAUKEE BARBECUE SAUCE

1 14-ounce bottle ketchup
1 cup beer
2 tablespoons brown sugar
2 tablespoons sugar
2 tablespoons Worcestershire
   sauce
1 cup chopped onion
1 teaspoon chili powder
   Dash of cayenne pepper,
   (optional)

Blend all ingredients together in small saucepan and bring to boiling point. In separate pan, brown meat to be served; cover with sauce and simmer in covered pan until meat is tender. Makes 1½ pints.

During the reign of Henry VIII, it appears there was a shortage of drinkable water and beer was consumed in large quantities. The ladies of the court were allotted a gallon of beer for breakfast.

BREWED BARBECUE SAUCE

1   14-ounce bottle ketchup
1   cup chili sauce
6   tablespoons prepared mustard
3/4   cup cider vinegar
1/2   cup lemon juice
1/4   cup A-1 steak sauce
2   tablespoons Worcestershire sauce
2   teaspoons soy sauce
1   tablespoon vegetable oil
1   12-ounce can beer
1   tablespoon black pepper
2   cloves garlic, crushed

Blend all ingredients together and keep in refrigerator until using on your favorite ribs, burgers, or steak. Makes 1 quart.

Brewing beer is a very sophisticated process. The ingredients barley, hops, and yeast must be carefully blended and balanced to achieve an individuality of taste.

140

TANGY BARBECUE SAUCE

1 cup chili sauce
3/4 cup beer
3 tablespoons soy sauce
3 tablespoons vegetable oil
1 teaspoon brown sugar
1/2 teaspoon salt
2 teaspoons grated onion
1 teaspoon dry mustard
1/2 teaspoon Tabasco sauce

Blend all ingredients together, mixing well. Keep in refrigerator until ready to use. Makes 1 pint.

If you have just bought your friend a glass of beer and he says he will get the "other half," he is saying he will buy you a drink in return.

BEER SAUCE

½ cup beer
2 tablespoons lemon juice
2 cups mayonnaise
½ cup ketchup
1 teaspoon prepared
   horseradish
2 tablespoons prepared
   mustard

Combine all ingredients, mixing well. Chill until ready to use. Excellent with seafood, especially shrimp. Makes 3 cups.

The Beer Institute, a national trade association, was founded in 1986. In addition to its work as legislative liaison, the Institute works with civic and charitable groups throughout the country to support safety and moderation campaigns.

142

TOUCH O' BREW SAUCE

1½ cups chili sauce
¼ cup butter or margarine, melted
2 tablespoons brown sugar
1 tablespoon dried onion flakes
½ teaspoon salt
½ teaspoon crushed red pepper
1 12-ounce can beer, divided
1 tablespoon cornstarch

In medium saucepan, combine all ingredients except ¼ cup beer and cornstarch. Bring sauce to a boil; reduce heat and simmer 10-15 minutes. In a small bowl, combine remaining beer and cornstarch. Add small amount of hot mixture to beer/cornstarch, stir well, and return all to saucepan. Continue stirring until mixture comes to a boil.

Best if made ahead to this point; cool, cover, and refrigerate up to 24 hours to allow flavors to blend. Use in any barbecued dish or as a sauce on ribs and hamburger. Can be stored in refrigerator up to 2 weeks. Makes 1½ pints.

The per-capita consumption of beer in the Czech Republic is over 140 quarts a year; they are among the world's beer drinking champions.

143

BEER MORNAY SAUCE

1/2 cup butter
1 cup flour
3 cups milk
2 pounds Velveeta cheese, shredded
1 12-ounce can beer

Melt butter in saucepan; add flour to make roux as for cream sauce. Slowly add milk. Add cheese, stirring constantly until cheese melts. Add beer, stirring constantly until smooth. Keep in refrigerator. Makes 1 1/2 quarts.

Today we take for granted the beer can with its easily opened tab; however, this convenience has only been around since 1962.

144

BEER MUSTARD

1/2 cup Chinese mustard
    powder
1/4 cup white vinegar
 1 cup flat beer
 2 teaspoons brown sugar
1/4 teaspoon salt
 3 egg yolks

Blend all ingredients except egg yolks together in glass bowl and let stand overnight. Transfer to top of double boiler over lightly boiling water. Add egg yolks one at a time, stirring with wire whisk. Stir mixture constantly until mustard is thick. Remove from heat and store in refrigerator. Can be kept up to 3 weeks. Makes 2 1/2 cups.

"Flip," a popular drink during Colonial days, was beer and gin mixed together with beaten egg whites and sugar, then "flipped" from one pitcher to another and topped with nutmeg.

HOT BACON DRESSING

1   **pound bacon, diced**
1/2 **cup cider vinegar**
2   **teaspoons dry mustard**
1/2 **cup diced onion**
1   **cup brown sugar**
1   **cup beer**
2 1/2 **tablespoons flour**

Fry bacon to a golden brown; remove from skillet and set aside. Leave scant covering of grease in bottom of skillet. Add vinegar, dry mustard, onion, and sugar and heat over medium heat. Combine beer and flour and add to skillet. Cook dressing until thickened, 6-8 minutes. Add reserved bacon pieces. Serve hot dressing over fresh spinach salad or salad of choice. This dressing is also delicious served over French cut green beans. Serves 6-8.

Light beers have some 30 percent fewer calories than regular beer—they average 8 calories per ounce to 12 calories per ounce for regular.

DESSERTS

147-168

CHOCOLATE SHEET CAKE

2 cups flour
2 cups sugar
1 cup margarine
1 cup beer
3 tablespoons cocoa
2 eggs
1 teaspoon baking soda
1/2 cup buttermilk
1 teaspoon vanilla

Sift together flour and sugar; set aside. Mix margarine, beer, and cocoa in saucepan and bring to a boil. Pour over flour mixture and blend well. In smaller bowl, beat eggs. Add baking soda, buttermilk, and vanilla; mix well. Add to large bowl and mix well. Pour into greased 10 x 15-inch sheet pan. Bake for approximately 20-25 minutes, until cake tester comes out clean. Frost with Cocoa-Beer Frosting. Serves 20-25.

COCOA-BEER FROSTING

1/2 cup margarine, softened
3 1/2 cups powdered sugar
1/3 cup cocoa
1 teaspoon vanilla
1/3 cup beer (approximately)

Combine margarine, powdered sugar, cocoa, and vanilla. Beat until smooth, adding sufficient beer to make mixture of spreading consistency.

148

CHOCOLATE BUNDT CAKE

1 18.25-ounce package
   milk chocolate cake mix
1 .09-ounce package instant
   chocolate pudding and
   pie filling
4 eggs
1¼ cups beer
½ cup oil
1 6-ounce package chocolate
   chips
   Powdered sugar

Place cake mix, dry pudding, eggs, beer, and oil in a large bowl. With an electric mixer, blend on low speed, then beat at medium speed until well blended. Fold in chocolate chips. Put mixture in well-greased and floured Bundt pan and bake at 350 degrees for 50-55 minutes. Cool upright in pan fifteen minutes. Turn upside down on plate until it releases itself. Dust with powdered sugar. Serves 10-12.

Malt liquor is brewed in a bottom-fermentation process; this beer has a higher alcoholic content than regular beer. The taste is aromatic and malty.

Today a "six pack" is a common expression; however, beer in cans was only introduced in 1935.

149

PEANUT BUTTER AND BEER CAKE

2 cups sugar
2 cups flour
1 cup margarine
1/4 cup cocoa
1 cup beer
1 teaspoon baking soda
1/2 cup sour milk (buttermilk
    can be substituted)
2 eggs
1 teaspoon vanilla
1 1/2 cups peanut butter

In large bowl, combine sugar and flour. In saucepan, combine margarine, cocoa, and beer; bring to a boil. Add to flour mixture. In small bowl, mix soda, sour milk, eggs, and vanilla together and add to beer mixture. Pour into greased and floured 9 x 13-inch cake pan and bake in 350-degree oven for 25 minutes or until cake tester comes out clean. When cake is completely cool, spread peanut butter on top. (To make spreading easier you can wet knife with warm water or mix small amount of peanut oil with peanut butter.) Frost with Chocolate Frosting. Serves 12-16.

CHOCOLATE FROSTING

2 tablespoons cocoa
2 tablespoons margarine
2 tablespoons Karo syrup
2 tablespoons beer
2 cups powdered sugar

Mix all ingredients except powdered sugar together; add powdered sugar. Beat with electric mixer until smooth. Spread evenly over peanut butter.

150

CHERRY CAKE

3 cups flour
2 teaspoons baking soda
1/2 teaspoon salt
3/4 cup margarine
2 cups sugar
2 eggs, lightly beaten
2 ounces chocolate, melted
1 cup cold beer
3/4 cup buttermilk
1 10-ounce jar maraschino cherries, drained and chopped; reserve juice
3/4 cup chopped nuts

Sift flour, soda, and salt together; set aside. In large mixing bowl, cream margarine and sugar until fluffy; add eggs and melted chocolate. Add sifted dry ingredients alternately with beer, buttermilk, and reserved cherry juice. Add cherries and nuts. Bake in greased and floured 9x13-inch cake pan for 40 minutes or until cake tester comes out clean. Serves 12-16.

Beer is the drink for you if you are real thirsty and watching calories. A 3-ounce whiskey is 195 calories, a 3-ounce after-dinner liqueur is 300 calories, and a 12-ounce beer is only 144 calories.

POPPY SEED-LEMON-BEER CAKE

1   18.25-ounce box deluxe yellow cake mix
1   3-ounce package vanilla instant pudding
5   tablespoons poppy seeds
1/2   cup vegetable oil
1   cup beer
4   eggs
1   teaspoon vanilla

In large bowl, combine cake mix, pudding mix, and poppy seeds; mix well. Add vegetable oil and beer and mix with electric beater for 2 minutes at medium speed. Add eggs one at a time, mixing well after each addition. Add vanilla and mix at high speed for one minute. Pour into well-greased and floured 9x13-inch pan and bake for 30 minutes or until cake tester comes out clean. Spread warm cake with Lemon-Beer Sauce. Cool and frost with whipped topping or whipped cream. Serves 12-16.

LEMON-BEER SAUCE

1/2   cup sugar
2   tablespoons cornstarch
1   cup beer
2   tablespoons margarine
3   tablespoons lemon rind, grated
3   tablespoons lemon juice
1-2   drops yellow food coloring

In 1-quart saucepan, combine sugar and cornstarch; gradually stir in beer. Stirring constantly, cook over medium heat until mixture comes to boil. Boil and stir for one minute. Remove from heat and add margarine, lemon rind, lemon juice, and yellow food coloring. Spread on cake.

ORANGE PINEAPPLE CAKE

1 18.25-ounce package
   yellow cake mix
1 1/3 cups beer
 1/3 cup oil
3 eggs
1 11-ounce can mandarin
   oranges, drained

Blend cake mix, beer, oil, and eggs in large bowl at low speed until moistened. Beat at medium speed for 2 minutes. Add mandarin oranges and pour into two greased and floured 9-inch cake pans. Bake at 350 degrees for 30 minutes or until cake tester comes out clean. Cool on rack for 15 minutes; remove from pans and cool completely. Frost with Pineapple Frosting. Serves 10-12.

PINEAPPLE FROSTING

1 16-ounce container Cool Whip
1 20-ounce can crushed
   pineapple, well-drained

Mix Cool Whip and pineapple together and frost between layers, top and sides.

The ideal temperature for storing beer is 45 degrees Fahrenheit; if too cold it becomes flat and cloudy.

BEER BARREL CAKE

1 cup margarine
6 tablespoons cocoa
1 cup beer
2 cups flour
2 cups sugar
1 teaspoon soda
1/2 cup buttermilk
2 eggs, beaten
1 teaspoon vanilla
1 1/2 cups miniature
    marshmallows

Heat margarine, cocoa, and beer to boiling. Pour over flour, sugar, and soda. Mix well. Add buttermilk, eggs, vanilla, and marshmallows. Pour into greased and floured 9 x 13 -inch pan. Bake at 350 degrees for 30-35 minutes. Frost with Beer Barrel Frosting. Serves 12-16.

BEER BARREL FROSTING

1/2 cup margarine
4 tablespoons cocoa
6 tablespoons beer
1 cup miniature
    marshmallows
2 2/3 cups powdered sugar,
    sifted
1 teaspoon vanilla
1 cup chopped nuts

Bring margarine, cocoa, and beer to boil. Add marshmallows, stirring until dissolved. Add powdered sugar, vanilla, and nuts. Frost cake while it is still warm. Cake and frosting may be frozen.

154

BEER CAKE WITH LEMON GLAZE

1   cup shortening
2   cups brown sugar
2   eggs, beaten
3   cups flour
1/2 teaspoon salt
2   teaspoons soda
1   teaspoon cinnamon
1/2 teaspoon allspice
1/2 teaspoon cloves
2   cups beer
1   cup walnuts or pecans,
      chopped
2   cups dates or prunes,
      finely chopped

Cream shortening and sugar until fluffy; beat in eggs. Sift flour, salt, soda, and spices together. Reserve 2 tablespoons dry mixture and add remainder to batter. Slowly add beer—this will foam, but that's all right.

Toss nuts and fruit into reserved flour mixture to coat and stir into batter.

Bake in greased and floured 10-inch Bundt or tube pan at 350 degrees for 1 1/4 hours. Cool in pan for 10 minutes then turn out to completely cool. Frost with Lemon Glaze. Serves 10.

LEMON GLAZE

1 1/2 cups powdered sugar,
        sifted
   4 tablespoons lemon juice

Mix sugar and lemon juice together—mixture will be thin. Drizzle over top and sides of cake.

155

SPICY BEER CAKE

1 12-ounce can beer
1 cup quick oats
2/3 cup margarine
1 cup sugar
1 cup brown sugar, packed
2 eggs
1 1/4 teaspoons vanilla
1 3/4 cup flour
1 1/4 teaspoons soda
1 1/2 teaspoons cinnamon
1/2 teaspoon nutmeg
1 cup finely chopped nuts

Bring beer to boiling point in saucepan. Add oats and let stand 20 minutes. In a separate bowl, cream margarine and sugars together; blend in eggs and vanilla. Add oatmeal mixture and mix well. Sift dry ingredients and add to creamed mixture; add nuts. Pour into greased and floured 9x13-inch cake pan. Bake at 350 degrees for 35 minutes or until cake tester comes out clean. While cake is still warm to the touch, frost with Broiled Caramel Frosting. Serves 12-16.

BROILED CARAMEL FROSTING

1/2 cup margarine
1 cup dark brown sugar, packed
1 cup flaked coconut
2 tablespoons half-and-half

Combine all ingredients and mix well. Spread on cake and broil on lowest rack until bubbly and golden brown.

APPLE CRUMB CAKE

2 cups sifted flour
1 cup brown sugar, packed
1/2 cup quick-cooking oats
3/4 cup butter or margarine,
   melted
1 cup sugar
3 tablespoons cornstarch
1 cup beer
1 teaspoon vanilla
6 medium apples, peeled

Mix flour, brown sugar, oats, and melted butter together until crumbs form. Place half of the crumbs in bottom of 13x9x2-inch cake pan. In a saucepan mix sugar, cornstarch, and beer. Cook until thickened, stirring constantly; add vanilla. Thinly slice peeled apples and add to mixture, gently stirring to get all apple pieces coated. Spread apple mixture over crumb layer and sprinkle remaining crumb mixture on top, gently pressing down. Bake for 50-55 minutes at 350 degrees. Serves 12-16.

New microbreweries are springing up from coast to coast. They share a common heritage with many large American brewers who started out in much the same way over 125 years ago.

157

RAISIN BEER CAKE

1 cup margarine
1 cup plus 2 tablespoons
   brown sugar
2 eggs, well beaten
4 cups flour
1 teaspoon baking soda
1 cup raisins
1 12-ounce can beer

Cream margarine and sugar until fluffy; add eggs. Combine flour and baking soda and add to creamed mixture. Add raisins and stir in beer. Spoon into greased 9x13-inch cake pan and smooth top with back of spoon. Bake at 350 degrees for 30 minutes or until cake tester comes out clean. Serves 12-16.

A clay tablet found in Nineveh, dated approximately 2000 B.C., indicates that beer was one of the provisions aboard Noah's ark.

The art of brewing beer was practiced in the New World by Indians long before the discoveries of Christopher Columbus. The first Europeans to brew beer in America were the Virginia Colonists in the year 1587.

158

GINGER BREAD

1 cup beer
1 cup margarine, softened
1 cup brown sugar
1 cup molasses
3 eggs, beaten
3 cups flour
1 teaspoon baking powder
1 teaspoon baking soda
1/2 teaspoon salt
1 1/2 teaspoons ginger
1 1/2 teaspoons cinnamon

Bring beer to boil. In large mixing bowl, pour beer over margarine. Add sugar, molasses, and eggs. Sift together flour, baking powder, baking soda, salt, and spices. Add to beer mixture, beating with electric beater until smooth.

Pour batter into greased and floured 9 x 13-inch cake pan. Bake in 350-degree oven for approximately 35 minutes, until cake tester comes out clean. Serve with Lemon Sauce. Serves 12-16.

LEMON SAUCE

1/2 cup sugar
2 tablespoons cornstarch
1 cup beer
2 tablespoons margarine
2 tablespoons grated lemon rind
2 tablespoons lemon juice
1-2 drops yellow food coloring

Over medium heat, in 1-quart saucepan, combine sugar and cornstarch; gradually stir in beer. Stirring constantly, cook until mixture comes to boil; boil and stir for one minute. Remove from heat and add margarine, lemon rind, lemon juice, and food coloring. Can be served hot or cold.

159

BEER CHEESECAKE

1½ cups zwieback, crushed

1¾ cups plus 3 tablespoons sugar, divided

6 tablespoons butter, melted

32 ounces cream cheese, softened

2 cups cheddar cheese, softened to room temperature

3 tablespoons flour

5 eggs

3 egg yolks

¼ cup beer

Apple slices, garnish (dip in lemon juice to avoid darkening)

Blend zwieback crumbs, 3 tablespoons sugar, and butter in small bowl. Press firmly over the bottom and partly up the side of a lightly buttered 9-inch springform pan; refrigerate until ready to fill.

Preheat oven to 475 degrees. In a large bowl, beat cream cheese and cheddar cheese with electric beater just until smooth. Add remaining sugar and flour; beat until light and fluffy. Add eggs and egg yolks one at a time, beating well after each addition. Stir in beer. Pour into crumb crust.

Bake for 12 minutes; lower temperature to 250 degrees and bake for 1½ hours. Turn oven off; let cake remain in oven for 1 hour. Remove from oven; cool completely on wire rack. Cake may crack on top, but it is the nature of the cake and will not affect flavor. Loosen around edge with a knife; release spring and remove side of pan, leaving cake on bottom. Top with apple slices, if desired. Serves 8-10.

BEER AND PRETZEL CHOCOLATE PIE

1 cup crushed pretzels
1/2 cup sugar
1/3 cup butter, melted
1 31/4-ounce package
   chocolate pie filling
   (not instant)
1 cup evaporated milk
1 cup beer
   Cool Whip

Prepare crust by combining pretzel crumbs, sugar, and butter; blend well. Press into 9-inch pie plate and bake at 400 degrees for 10 minutes. Set aside and cool.

In saucepan, combine chocolate pie filling, milk, and beer; cook over medium heat until mixture comes to a rolling boil. Remove from heat, stirring occasionally for 5-10 minutes. Pour into pie crust and chill in refrigerator. Just before serving, spread Cool Whip on top. Serves 6-8.

According to an University of Pennsylvania study, 83 percent of the 500 women surveyed consider themselves to be beer drinkers. Thirty-six percent of the women drink seven or more glasses a week. What's more, 75 percent of the beer drinking women did not perceive beer to be a male associated beverage.

CHOCOLATE BEER PIE

3 eggs
1/3 cup flour
3/4 cup plus 3 tablespoons
    sugar, divided
3 tablespoons cocoa
1 cup beer
1 cup milk
1 teaspoon vanilla
1 tablespoon butter
1 9-inch pie shell, baked

Separate eggs. Slightly beat yolks; set egg whites in refrigerator for meringue.

Mix flour, sugar, and cocoa together in heavy saucepan. Over low to medium heat, gradually add beer and then milk. When smooth, add egg yolks. Cook until mixture thickens, stirring constantly. Remove from heat, cool and add vanilla and butter. Pour into pie shell.

Make a meringue topping by whipping reserved egg whites until stiff. Gradually add remaining sugar while continuing to whip. Spread meringue on pie in peaks and mounds. Place in 400-degree oven for approximately 5-7 minutes, until meringue is lightly browned. Serves 6-8.

Beer is extolled in the Egyptian Book of the Dead, where the varieties of beer listed include "beer of truth" and "beer of eternity."

LEMON MERINGUE PIE

1½ cups plus 3 tablespoons sugar
6 tablespoons cornstarch
3 cups beer
6 tablespoons margarine
6 tablespoons grated lemon rind
6 tablespoons lemon juice
1-3 drops yellow food coloring
1 9-inch pie shell, baked
3 egg whites

In large saucepan, over low to medium heat, combine 1½ cups sugar and cornstarch; mix well and gradually stir in beer. Stirring constantly, cook over medium heat until mixture comes to boil; boil and stir for 1 minute. Remove from heat and add margarine, lemon rind, lemon juice, and food coloring. Cool and pour into baked pie shell.

To make meringue, whip egg whites until stiff. Gradually add remaining 3 tablespoons sugar, continuing to whip. Spread on pie top in peaks and mounds. Place in 400-degree oven for about 5 minutes. Serves 6-8.

Ale is a rapidly fermented beer (top-fermented), providing a robust taste. Ale is fermented from wort at warm temperatures (58-70 degrees).

163

BAKED APPLES

4 large cooking apples
½ cup brown sugar
½ cup sugar
1 cup beer
1 tablespoon margarine
½ teaspoon cinnamon
2-3 drops red food coloring

Core apples and peel about one-third down from top. Arrange, peeled side up, in an ungreased cake pan. In saucepan, mix brown and white sugars, beer, margarine, cinnamon, and food coloring. Bring to boil and continue boiling for about 5 minutes to form syrup. Pour over apples and bake uncovered for 1 hour. Serve hot or cold topped with whipped cream or ice cream.

Hops are vine-like plants with cone-shaped cluster blossoms that add spice to beer, giving it a special aroma, flavor, and character.

On April 7, 1933, the headline of the New York Times *read "Beer Flows in 19 States at Midnight," announcing that Prohibition was over. In reality, it was legalized in 20 states and the District of Columbia; in December of that year the 21st Amendment was ratified to the Constitution effecting a national repeal of Prohibition.*

APPLE FRITTERS

1 cup flour
1 cup beer, divided
4-6 apples (approximately
    1½ pounds)
    Oil for deep frying
    Powdered sugar

Blend flour with ⅔ cup beer and beat with wire whisk until smooth; add balance of beer. The batter will be similar to a heavy, thick syrup; let stand for at least 1 hour.

Peel and core apples and slice approximately ⅜-inch thick. Put apple slices into batter and cover each slice completely.

In deep skillet heat one to two inches of oil to 350 degrees. Slide 2 to 3 coated apple sliced into hot oil; cook only a few fritters at a time. Fry fritters approximately 90 seconds on each side. Lift fritters out with slotted spoon and drain on paper towel. Sprinkle with powdered sugar. Serves 6.

A 1600 B.C. medical handbook lists beer as an ingredient in over one hundred medicines used at that time.

BEER SORBET

1½ cups sugar
¾ cup water
2 12-ounce cans beer
2 tablespoons lemon juice
2 tablespoons orange juice

Make simple syrup by combining sugar and water in small saucepan. Bring to boiling point; reduce heat and simmer for 5 minutes. Let syrup cool to room temperature and combine with beer, orange and lemon juices.

Put mixture into metal freezer trays and freeze until mixture begins to crystallize. Spoon into large stainless steel mixing bowl and beat with electric beater until smooth. Return to freezer trays and refreeze until mixture again forms ice crystals. Remove and, again using electric beater, whip until smooth. Put mixture into bowl and return to freezer until frozen completely.

This sorbet can be used as a dessert, but it also can be served between courses to cleanse the palate, especially after Italian or Mexican food. Makes 3 pints.

BEER FUDGE

3 ounces (3 squares)
   unsweetened chocolate
4 cups sugar
   Pinch of salt
1 cup beer
2 tablespoons margarine
1 teaspoon vanilla
1 cup chopped nuts

In large saucepan, combine chocolate, sugar, salt, beer, and margarine and mix well. Cook over medium heat until chocolate and butter are melted, stirring so sugar and beer are mixed in well. Bring to a boil and continue to boil to 230-240 degrees on candy thermometer. (If you do not have candy thermometer, boil to a soft ball stage.) Cool thoroughly. Add vanilla and nuts and beat until mixture loses its shine. Be careful not to beat fudge too long or it will not spoon out into pan. Pour into greased 9x9-inch pan. Cut into pieces while still soft. Serves 16-20.

Some historians believe that in the early ages, the harvesting of grains was not for the primary use of making bread; rather it was to have the ingredient for making beer. Beer and bread originate from the same root word "brot."

167

BEER BALLS

1 cup semi-sweet chocolate
   chips
3 tablespoons dark corn syrup
1/2 cup beer
1 cup crushed vanilla wafer
   cookies (approximately
   22 cookies)
1/2 cup powdered sugar
1 cup chopped nuts
   Granulated sugar

In mixing bowl, melt chocolate chips in microwave; blend in syrup and beer. Add cookies, powdered sugar, and nuts. Mix well. Let cool about 30 minutes, until cool enough to handle. Form into 1-inch balls and roll in granulated sugar. Makes 2 dozen.

Beer and breweries around the world have been named in the honor of King Gambrinus, often referred to as the patron saint of brewers. In fact, Gambrinus was neither king nor saint. The name is a corruption of Jan Primus, a medieval German duke who was made an honorary member of the Cologne brewers' guild in 1288.

This is just a brief list of the many sources that have provided useful information for this book. Some bits and pieces of knowledge could not be traced to their precise origin and, therefore, remain "anonymous."

Baron, Stanley. Brewed in America: *A History of Beer and Ale in the United States.* Massachusetts: Little Brown and Co., 1962.

Beer Institute. "Continuing the Great Tradition of Beer." Washington D.C., 1989.

Birmingham, Frederic. *Falstaffs Complete Beer Book.* New York: Universal-Award House, Inc., 1970.

Brown, Sanborn C. *Wines & Beers of Old New England.* New Hampshire: The University Press of New England, 1978.

Lipp, Martin R., M.D. *The I Like My Beer Diet.* New York: M. Evans and Company, Inc. 1984.

Weiner, Michael A. *The Taster's Guide to Beer.* New York: MacMillan Publishing Co., Inc., 1977.

INDEX OF RECIPES